Emily Post on Guests and Hosts

EMILY POST

on

Guests and Hosts

Elizabeth L. Post

HarperPerennial
A Division of HarperCollinsPublishers

HarperCollins books may be purchased for educational, business, or sales promotional use. For information address HarperCollinsPublishers, Inc. 10 East 53rd Street, New York, New York 10022.

FIRST EDITION

ISBN 0-06-274009-1 (pbk)
    96 97 98 ◆/OPM 10 9 8 7 6 5 4 3 2

Contents

Introduction

"If a guest prefers to sit on the veranda and read, don't interrupt him every half page to ask if he really does not want to do something else. If, on the other hand, a guest wants to exercise, don't do everything in your power to obstruct his starting off by saying that it will surely rain, or that it is too hot, or that you think it is senseless to spend days that should be a rest to him in utterly exhausting himself." Emily Post wrote these words in 1922. Nothing has changed. Perhaps we seldom hear the word veranda anymore, but the sentiment is exactly the same today.

The considerate guest is all that he or she was in 1922, and more, whether invited for an hour for a cup of coffee, or for the weekend or longer. The considerate host or hostess has planned so carefully that she or he is relaxed and able to enjoy the company of his or her invited guests while neither badgering them with too much attention nor dashing, frazzled, hither and thither, making them feel like terrible burdens.

Over the years, the art of being a gracious host and the skill of being a perfect guest have been presented with new challenges. Does one serve invited guests mineral shakes because one is on a diet? Does a telephone invitation, more immediate than a written one, require an immediate response? Other questions are seemingly age-old, but never have been addressed in etiquette books before, giving way to more usual queries having to do with form and formalities. What do I do with my wet towel when visiting a friend who has no towel racks free? What do I do when everyone can't reach the cheese and crackers on my coffee table? Who writes a thank-you note to my husband's boss for an evening entertainment...does he, as the employee, or do I, because I always write our thank-you notes?

These questions are among almost 250 others in this book that have been asked of me by past, present and future guests and hosts who wish their entertaining and visiting moments to be worry-free, comfortable and correct. Although my answers are specific to the questions asked, the universal answer is that treating others with thoughtfulness and courtesy—no matter their age, calling in life or social skills—is what matters most. The most sought-after guests are those who bring with them their sunniest smiles and most willing natures. The hosts whose invitations are cherished are those who know how to make their guests comfortable in a seemingly effortless way. Mutual respect is more than half of what comprises the essence of the best-loved guests and hosts.

If thoughtfulness, respect, courtesy and caring are your traits already, you may not need this book as the answers will come to you naturally. Even so, there are details you may wish to add to your hosting and guesting ability and for everyone, experienced or not, I hope it will provide you with the answers to some of your thorniest questions as you continue to be everyone's favorite guest and host.

Elizabeth L. Post
1994

R.S.V.P.

Q. *How far in advance should I invite guests to a dinner party?*
A. Invitations should be issued anywhere from two to four weeks in advance, depending on the formality of the dinner party. The more formal the dinner, the more advance notice you should provide.

Q. *Are there any rules governing what kind of invitation I send for a dinner party?*
A. The kind of invitation you send depends on the kind of party you are having. You may use formal, third-person invitations for the most formal dinner parties, and issue invitations by telephone for spontaneous informal dinners with close friends. Invitations for dinner parties that are informal may be purchased fill-in invitations or written on fold-over notepaper.

Q. *What does a third-person formal invitation look like?*
A. A formal invitation is engraved or printed on white or cream cards, either plain or plate-marked, or it is handwritten on personal notepaper.

The typeface is a matter of personal choice. The store where you order your invitations will have samples to show you.

Punctuation is used only when words requiring separation occur on the same line and in such abbreviations as R.s.v.p. The time is never given as nine-thirty, but as half after nine o'clock or half past nine o'clock.

If the event is to be given at one address and the hostess lives at another, her address should appear below the R.S.V.P., assuming that she wishes replies to go to her home.

If the party is formal, the phrase "black tie" or "white tie" appears in the lower right-hand corner of the invitation.

Q. *If I want to use a formal, third-person invitation, is there an alternative to having the entire invitation engraved or printed?*
A. Yes, you can order printed third-person fill-in invitations from the stationer that leave blanks for specific information and which can be used for any number of occasions. These generally look like this:

---

request the pleasure of the company of

at

on

at

R.S.V.P.

Q. *Are titles used on formal invitations?*
A. Yes, always. The title "Miss" is not used on formal wedding invitations before the bride's name, but is used on all other formal invitations.

Q. *How do handwritten formal invitations differ from engraved invitations?*

A. They vary little. The wording and spacing must follow exactly as they would if the invitation were engraved. The cream or white paper used may be plain or it may include a very small monogram, but it may never be headed by an address. If the family has a crest or coat of arms, it may be stamped, without color, on the invitation.

Q. *I'm sometimes confused about what to write on invitations that I buy at the stationery store. What should be written after the word "for"?*
A. The "for" leads to your writing "cocktails and dinner," or "swimming and a barbecue," or "a luncheon in honor of Mary Brown," or whatever the occasion is to which you are issuing invitations.

Q. *When there is no printed "R.S.V.P." on a purchased invitation, may I write it in? Is it appropriate to ask recipients to call with their response and add my telephone number?*
A. Yes, you may write in the letters "R.S.V.P.," followed by your telephone number. It is more customary, except when the event is a most formal dinner party, for people to respond by telephone rather than in writing.

Q. *What does "regrets" or "regrets only" mean on an invitation?*
A. This means that you are to respond to the invitation only when you are unable to attend. Otherwise it is assumed that you are accepting the invitation.

Q. How is a formal reply worded?
A. The general rule is "reply in kind." Once learned, the formal reply is the easiest to write, because it is written in the same form as the invitation, substituting the order of names. The reply should be written in the third-person form if that is the style of the invitation. In accepting the invitation you must repeat the day and hour so that any mistake can be rectified. But if you decline an invitation it is not necessary to repeat the hour.

If the invitation reads:

> *Mr. and Mrs. Arthur Mignone*
> *request the pleasure of your company*
> *at dinner*
> *on Saturday, the twelfth of June*
> *at half past seven o'clock*
> *20 Seagate Road*
> *Darien, Connecticut 06820*
> *R.s.v.p.*

the acceptance reply would read:

> *Mr. and Mrs. Robert Werner*
> *accept with pleasure*
> *the kind invitation of*
> *Mr. and Mrs. Arthur Mignone*
> *for dinner*
> *on Saturday, the twelfth of June*
> *at half past seven o'clock*

Another option, which is not quite so formal, is:

Mr. and Mrs. Frank Kilduff
accept with pleasure
Mr. and Mrs. Mignone's
kind invitation for dinner
on Saturday, the twelfth of June
at half past seven o'clock

The formula for regretting the invitation reads:

Mr. and Mrs. Richard King
regret that they are unable to accept
the kind invitation of
Mr. and Mrs. Arthur Mignone
for Saturday, the twelfth of June

or, equally acceptable:

Mr. and Mrs. Lawrence Wong
regret that they are unable to accept
Mr. and Mrs. Mignone's
kind invitation for dinner
on Saturday, the twelfth of June

Q. *When a friend calls and invites us to dinner, do I have to give an answer right away? Is it impolite to ask if I can check and call her back?*
A. No, you needn't give an immediate answer, but you should get back to her within a day with your response. When the invitation is extended, say, "That sounds wonderful! I have to check my calendar and George's schedule to make sure he's going to be in town. I'll call you tonight (or tomorrow) with our answer.

Q. We received an invitation on a commercial fill-in card worded in the third person. Do we reply as if it were a formal invitation?

A. No, even though the wording is third-person, this is not a formal invitation and need not be answered as such. A brief note or a telephone call (if the number appears on the invitation), or your own informal or notepaper with "So very sorry, must regret the 10th," or "Looking forward to the 10th with pleasure," is all that is necessary.

Q. If I am invited to a dinner party and don't wish to attend, do I then have to refuse another invitation that I would like to accept for the same evening?

A. You must exercise discretion in the way you handle this. You certainly may refuse any invitation, but in declining the first invitation you should not make up an excuse, as in, "William will be out of town," when William is going nowhere, or "Thank you, but we have theater tickets," when you really don't. If you decline by saying, "We're so sorry we cannot accept your invitation, but we already have other plans—thank you for thinking of us," you are free to accept another invitation without causing yourself an embarrassing situation should you happen to run into the person who issued the first invitation.

Q. We are having weekend guests and have been invited to a dinner party in the neighborhood. Is it permissible to ask the dinner party hostess to extend an invitation to our guests?

A. No, it is not. When regretting an invitation because you have guests yourself, you should explain your reason to the hostess. She then has the option to say, "I'm so sorry you won't be able to join us—we'll miss you!" or, if she is having a buffet or a cocktail party where one or two unexpected guests won't make a difference in her planning she may say, "Do bring them. I'd love to meet them."

Q. *When my roommate and I have a party, are we obligated to invite someone a friend is dating? What do we do if a friend accepts and asks if she can or should bring a date?*

A. No, you are not obligated to invite "dates," although you are obligated, when you are having a couples party, to invite someone with whom a friend is living since they are considered a permanent couple. When a friend asks if she can bring a date, your answer depends on the size of your party, the space you have available and whether you have invited other single guests. If you can accommodate another guest and have no reason to refuse, your answer would be yes. If your friend asks if she should bring a date, perhaps concerned that she would be the only person who wasn't part of a couple, your answer would be no, with the reassurance that there will be other single guests at the party.

Q. *Is it appropriate to include a list of suggested gifts in a shower invitation?*

A. The majority of the mail I receive on this topic

indicates that people are overwhelmingly offended when they feel they are being "told" what they should buy. However, it is quite appropriate to write "kitchen shower," "lingerie shower," or whatever it may be to indicate the general type of gifts expected. Although it is genuinely helpful to know what is needed or wanted, most people prefer to ask the hostess for specific ideas when they accept the invitation. The hostess should have a list handy for when guests do ask, with items in a range of prices. She should not, however, give the same suggestions to everyone who asks.

Q. *We are sponsoring a table at a charity dinner. How do I make it clear to those we invite that they will be our guests and are not expected to pay for their tickets?*
A. You say, "Charles and I would like you and Dan to be our guests at the Girls' Club dinner on the 27th." If the dinner is black tie, it is courteous to mention this as part of your invitation, since accepting the invitation obligates your potential guests to be appropriately attired—possibly at additional expense to themselves. It is also courteous to mention the others who will be joining you, as well as whether they should meet you at the dinner or whether you will be picking them up, etc. If you are sending the dinner invitation, you do not include a response card to the charity committee but rather write across the top, "Charles and I are hoping you will be our guests at this dinner—I'll call you next week to see if you can join us."

Q. How do I make it clear that I am inviting friends for dinner but am not planning to entertain their children, as well?

A. When you call or write, you say, "Tom and I are hoping you and John can get a sitter for Saturday night and come for dinner." This makes it quite clear that you are planning an adult evening without your having to say, "Don't bring the children!"

Q. What can I do when friends ask if they can bring their dog?

A. One assumes you would prefer that the dog does not attend the event you have invited your friends to enjoy. Whatever the reason, whether it be safety, your carpeting, feared harassment for your own pets, or allergies, you simply say, "No, I'm so sorry, but I just can't include Duke in the invitation—Terry's developed terrible allergies"; or, "I'm just not comfortable around dogs anymore"; or, "Buttons and Socks are just terrified when a dog is nearby and it takes them days to get over it." Even if your friend persists by assuring you that Duke is gentle, or flea-free or afraid to stay home alone, you have every right to persist, too, in your refusal to entertain uninvited pets of any sort.

Q. Should I ask people if they eat certain foods, like seafood or steak, when I invite them to dinner?

A. When you are inviting only a few people and you are planning to serve something unusual or something to which your guests may be allergic, such as seafood, you may say, "I was thinking of having a backyard clambake. . . does this sound fun to you, or are you or Chad not lobster and clam fans?" It is also all right to phrase your question, "I haven't planned my menu yet because I wanted to be sure there aren't any particular foods you can't or don't eat. . . ." This gives your guests the chance to tell you if they are vegetarians or on a no-salt diet, etc. When your dinner party is large, you would not ask your guests their preference but would assume there would be something on the menu that they would be able to eat.

Q. When guests offer to bring something to a dinner party should I say yes or not?
A. You certainly may say yes, if the party is a gathering of good friends who expect to participate by bringing a contribution toward dinner. You also should feel comfortable saying yes when you are having a cocktail party and a friend offers to bring an hors d'oeuvre. When your dinner party is large or formal, however, it is best to say, "Thank you so much, but please just bring yourselves." If guests are persistent, simply say, "Thank you for your wonderful offer, but the menu is all planned," or "I really appreciate your insisting, but Frank and I just want you to be here and relax and not do a thing."

Q. Do you think it is acceptable to put one general invitation on the bulletin board in the office when everyone is invited to a party?
A. It is acceptable, but it is not without its risks. The

invitation must be posted on a board that is for that department only so that readers from other offices know that the invitation is not intended for them. Otherwise you run the risk of having others think they are invited. If you do this, you should also post an R.S.V.P. sheet so that you know how many people are coming; otherwise you have no idea how to plan refreshments. To me, the real drawback is that this kind of invitation is impersonal and doesn't reflect much warmth or desire on your part that people actually attend. A personal invitation is far more sincere and is likely to generate a much better response.

Q. *What information should be included in an invitation for a weekend visit?*
A. A weekend invitation should be as clear as you can make it. It should include the time you would like your guests to arrive as well as when you would expect them to leave. It should also include any specific wardrobe needs—whites if tennis is in the offing; swimming suits if you are planning a day by the pool or at the beach; or formal wear if a particularly dressy evening is included. It should indicate the first meal you expect to serve them, as well as the last meal they should plan to have with you. If you are telephoning your invitation you might say something like this: "We are so hoping you will be able to join us at the shore the weekend of the 15th. If possible, plan to arrive for lunch on Friday (lunch is anytime between 12 and 2 when we're at the shore, so take your time), and stay through Sunday dinner. We try to have a late

afternoon dinner to give ourselves time to pack up and head home by 5, before the traffic becomes impossible. In between, if you and Larry still enjoy tennis, we can book a court for Saturday afternoon, and then Jim and I want to take you to dinner at the club. We have a new chef whose specialty is, as I recall, one of your favorites. Saturday night dinners are jacket and tie for the men; by the way, I usually wear a sundress (and bring a sweater because the evenings get cool). If the weather holds, there is nothing like a Sunday morning walk in the park followed by brunch and the Sunday paper on the deck, as casual and comfortable as we can get. Please say yes— it has been too long since the four of us have had a chance just to relax and catch up!"

Q. When I invite friends for the weekend, should I ask them if there is anything they want to do?
A. Doing this not only gives your guests the opportunity to let you know that they would love to have an afternoon of shopping at the outlets near you, but it also helps you to know how to plan. If, after they arrive, they tell you that they would like to visit the site of the Boston Tea Party and you have already bought tickets for OmniMax at the museum as a surprise treat, you can end up in quite a muddle.

Q. Is there a gracious way to extend an invitation for a weekend by mail, or should invitations be issued by telephone?
A. Although invitations usually are made by tele-

phone, they certainly may be written. An example would be:

> Dear Janine,
>
> Greg and I are hoping that you and Ted and the children can spend the Memorial Day weekend with us on Shelter Island. If Ted could leave the office a little early on Friday, the 29th, there is a 6:00 P.M. ferry that would get you here in time for dinner, and there are ferries leaving the island at 5:00 and 8:00 on Sunday evening. The fishing should be great, and the children are counting on Brendan and Laura for the annual picnic. Please come—we have wanted to show you the island for so long.
>
> Much love,
> Terry

Another example would be:

> Dear Peggy,
>
> The forecast is for snow and more snow, and Bob and I are hoping that you and Jack will spend the weekend after next skiing with us at Mt. Snow. Come as early as you can Friday, the sixth, and stay until Sunday night so as not to miss a minute of it. The Franklins are coming, too, so maybe you could drive up together. I'll give you directions when you call to say you are coming.

No formal clothes, only your ski outfits and something comfortable to change into after skiing. It's cold, so bring warm things. We'll get the passes—and if you don't want to drive up with your skis, the shop rents them for about $30 a weekend.

We're counting on you, so you have to say "Yes."

Love to you both,
Nicole

Q. *Some friends are notorious for always being very late. Should I tell them to arrive at an earlier hour than my other guests for an evening of dinner and theater? I'm afraid they will spoil the evening if we have to wait for them.*
A. You could do this, but be prepared for them to be on time for the first time in their lives! You could, instead, simply say, when they accept the invitation, that you are going to have to leave at 6 P.M. sharp or you will miss the show. Only the most thoughtless person will disregard this request for promptness, and unless these friends are thoroughly rude or not very bright, they surely will adhere to your schedule.

Q. *What do I do when people do not respond to an invitation? Is it all right to call them or is that rude?*
A. Of course you would not be rude to call. The rudeness is all theirs in not responding immediately. When you call, say, "Tom and I are so hoping you

and Brad will be able to join us on Saturday—I'm just checking to make sure you'll be with us." When an invitation has an actual R.S.V.P. deadline and you have not received a response, again, it is perfectly acceptable for you to call, particularly when the invitation is for an occasion where you have to let a caterer or restaurant know the number in your party.

Q. Some very good friends always try to attend my children's drama performances, but I feel like it is an imposition when the children ask them if they are coming. Should I buy their tickets in advance and give them to them after they have indicated that they will be there?
A. When you have specifically invited them, then you should plan to pay for their tickets. When they ask when a performance will be and indicate that they will be attending, on the other hand, you have no obligation to purchase tickets for them, although you may if you wish.

Q. I frequently receive invitations to fundraising events that have a handwritten note from a friend: "Hugh and I would love to have you join us at our table," or "Do hope you can attend this worthwhile event." Normally I would not respond to this kind of invitation if I wasn't planning on attending. Should I call or write a response when there is a personal note? Does this note mean they are inviting us to be their guests?
A. When invitations to large fundraisers are sent, it is usual for a group of members of the organization

sponsoring the event to meet, review mailing lists and do just what you have asked about—encourage attendance by personalizing the invitation. One person may write notes on literally dozens of invitations in hopes that friends will patronize the event. Unless there is a definite request for a response, there is no need to reply if you aren't attending. The personal note is not a "Be our guest" invitation. If it were, it would say so, and the envelope would not include a response card with the price of the tickets and directions on how to write your check.

If you do plan on attending, however, you would mail your response and money and then call your friend to say that you are attending and would love to be at her table if there is room.

Q. *Should I always offer to bring something when someone invites me to a dinner party at her home?*

A. If the invitation is to a true semiformal or formal dinner party, the answer to your question is no. If the invitation is by telephone and the evening is informal with just you or you and a few other friends, the answer is yes. In this case, instead of saying, "May I bring something," say, "What can I bring?"

Q. *If a cocktail party is held before a dinner dance or other function, may a guest accept the invitation to the party but not the dance?*

A. No, unless the hostess specifically says, "Please join us first even though you can't come to the dance afterward." In most cases, it is not up to you to make this suggestion. The only exception would be with very close friends where you might say, "I'd love to join you for a drink, but we are going to dinner at the Browns' that evening.

Q. *When someone has invited me to lunch a few times and I have not been able to make it and he finally says, "I really want to take you to lunch—call me with a date," I feel uncomfortable, thinking it sounds as though I'm looking for a free lunch if I call. What should I do?*
A. Assuming that you would enjoy having lunch with this person, you should call and let him know when you, indeed, are available. When you have had to refuse several invitations and then do not call as asked, you are indicating that you do not enjoy his company or do not wish to meet with him, not that you are uncomfortable about being his guest.

Q. *My husband and I were invited to dinner and the opera. He will be out of town, but I would love to go. Is it all right to accept for myself, or should I decline for both of us?*
A. Because tickets will have been ordered for two people, you must decline this invitation. Accepting would leave your hosts in the awkward position of "wasting" a ticket or of having to find another person to invite so that the ticket may be used. When regretting the invitation, you should say that you would love to accept and that the evening sounds heavenly, but that your husband will be traveling so you must

decline. Only if your hostess suggests that you attend anyway should you even consider it—you may not be the one to suggest it. This would be true for any other events that carry the expectation that you attend as a couple—balls or dances where you are invited to make up a table, an invitation to the theater and any occasions which involve tickets for a twosome. There are other occasions where it is appropriate to have one member of a couple accept and the other decline, including parties, bar or bat mitzvahs and weddings.

Q. *When invited for a weekend, what specifics should I include when responding?*
A. The thoughtful guest indicates his or her anticipated arrival time and departure time. In addition, a guest should let a host know, in advance, if she has other obligations while visiting or plans to visit another friend or if he will require several hours of quiet time for work he is bringing with him. If your host does not mention wardrobe needs or specific plans, you should ask what kinds of clothes you should bring. If a host asks if there is anything special you would like to do during your visit, and there is, this is the time to say so. This would include attending synagogue or church, touring a particular landmark or going for a swim.

Q. *My boss invited me to his country home for the weekend, along with several others from the office and their spouses. I am not married, but I am living* *with my boyfriend, which he may not know. Is it all right to ask for an invitation for him, too, or do I have to go by myself?*

A. It is all right to ask for an invitation for him, too, since invitations to pairs should always include living-together couples. See your boss privately and ask him, since you noticed that spouses were included in the invitation, if you may bring your boyfriend, with whom you live. He may say no if this arrangement somehow is not acceptable to him, although this is unlikely. If this does occur, you then have to choose whether to attend without your boyfriend or to decline the invitation.

Breakfast, Lunch, Dinner (and In-Between)

Q. *What do I do when a dinner guest brings something I wasn't expecting, like a cake for dessert, and I would prefer not to serve it?*

A. If the gift simply does not complement your dinner, you say, "Oh, thank you so much, Molly, this looks absolutely delicious—we'll all look forward to enjoying it tomorrow." If the guest inappropriately states that she brought it for *tonight,* you are free to tell her that you appreciate her intentions, but that since you weren't expecting a hazelnut torte, you already prepared a dessert and will be serving that, as planned. Naturally, if the gift does not interfere with your menu, and you would like to, you may serve it as part of your dinner.

Q. *When dinner guests arrive with wine, should I serve it instead of the wine I was planning to serve, or may I save it for another time?*

A. You may do whichever you wish. If you have carefully planned a wine that better complements your menu, you should thank your guest and say that you look forward to drinking their wine at a special time in the near future. If their wine complements your menu and is in a quantity sufficient to last through your dinner, there is no reason not to serve it if you want to.

Q. *I have just moved to a new neighborhood and am to be the guest of honor at a "get acquainted" coffee. Should I take a gift to my hostess?*

A. You should not take a gift with you. Instead, you

should either send flowers beforehand so your hostess has them for the party or send flowers or a small gift afterward, with a thank-you note.

Q. When one does take a hostess gift, what should it be and what should it not be?
A. There are very clear guidelines on what a hostess gift should *not* be. It should not be a surprise food item that you expect her to incorporate into her menu. Arriving with a chocolate cake when she already has planned a chocolate mousse for dessert is not helpful. It also should not be cut flowers that she must trim, find a vase for and arrange, unless you say, when presenting them, "These reminded us of you— lead me to a vase and I'll put them in water for you." And it should not be a bottle of wine with the comment, "Hope this goes with dinner!" A hostess gift may be a food item that has nothing to do with dinner—croissants and jam for her breakfast; a bottle of wine with the comment, "This is for you and Jim to enjoy some Friday night"; a box of candy. A hostess gift may be a flowering plant or a floral arrangement, and it may be a bottle of liquor, a book, a collection of crossword puzzles if your hostess is a fan or other small and thoughtful items.

Q. How do I know what to wear when I am invited to a dinner party?
A. You don't, unless your host specifies that the evening is casual or black tie or whatever. When the invitation is to the home of a friend, you generally

know whether their entertainments are of the jacket-and-tie and dress variety or the shorts and T-shirt type. When the invitation is to the home of a relative stranger, however, your apparel decision is more difficult. If you are really at a loss, you have to ask. "How formal is the evening, Sarah?" is your question, and she hopefully gives you a realistic answer. If you decide to make your own choice, you are probably safest with something that is neither too informal nor too dressy. It is far better to be underdressed than overdressed. Even when the invitation specifies a certain type of dress, it can be confusing. Let the following common terms and their meanings be your guide:

- "White tie" The most formal evening wear: white tie, wing collar and tailcoat. This is almost never required today, except for official and diplomatic occasions and a rare private ball.
- "Black tie" or "Formal" The ordinary formal evening wear: a tuxedo with soft shirt and bow tie. Formerly jackets were black, but today, especially in summer, they may be patterned and in almost any color.
- "Semiformal" On an invitation to a party, this means no jeans or T-shirts. Women wear dresses, skirts and blouses or "good" pants and tops—men wear sports shirts and slacks and perhaps a sports jacket.
- "Informal" or "casual" means just what it says. You should select something informal

and comfortable but neat, pressed and clean. Your attire should fit the occasion: for a poolside party, jeans and T-shirts would be fine.

Q. How long should dinner be delayed for a late guest?
A. Fifteen minutes is the established length of time. To wait more than 20 minutes, at the outside, would be showing rudeness to many for the sake of one. When the late guest finally arrives, he or she, of course, apologizes to the hostess and is then seated.

Q. We often invite a few friends to dinner and begin the evening with cocktails and hors d'oeuvres. Everyone can't reach the coffee table where I put things like crackers and cheese. Should I keep passing them, or expect our guests to get up and down every time they want something?
A. You should pass your hors d'oeuvres a few times to each guest and then leave the tray or platter on the table so guests can help themselves. Often, guests who are helping themselves will offer to slice cheese for another, or will take it upon themselves to pass a tray to others.

Q. Several times I have been a guest at someone's house, been given a cold drink, been seated in the living room and found no place to put my glass. There are no coasters in sight. May I just put the glass on the table, or should I hold it the whole time?
A. You should ask, "Carolyn, do you have a coaster

or something I can put my glass on? If she says, "Just put it right on the table," of course you may.

Q. *I'm always embarrassed to ask to use someone's bathroom when I am in their house. What should I say?*
A. There is nothing I know of that is particularly embarrassing about bathrooms. Everyone uses them, and if you have a need for one, you should just ask, "Jane, may I use your bathroom?" If you don't know where it is, you could ask, "Jane, could you point me in the direction of your bathroom?" If you just can't do this, then you can fabricate an excuse for needing it, such as to take out your contact lenses or to wash your hands.

Q. *When I use someone's bathroom and there are no guest towels, is it all right to use any towel that is there?*
A. Not really, but you sometimes have no choice but to do that, if your hostess has forgotten to put out guest towels. The alternative is to let your hands drip dry, which takes a considerable amount of time, or to dry them on your clothing, which is not satisfactory, either. Just be sure your hands are really clean, whether you are forced to use a family towel or are using a guest towel, so that you aren't wiping grime onto the towels.

Q. *There have been a few occasions when I have gone to use someone's bathroom and there is no toilet tissue. Is it rude to ask for some?*
A. Of course, it isn't rude. Harried hostesses, especially those with families who think nothing of using

the last of something and not replacing it, can over-look toilet tissue in their last-minute checklist of things to do. What is important is that you look for tissue *before* you have closeted yourself in the bath-room so that you aren't stuck in the predicament of being trapped and in need! Just find your hostess and say, "Fran, show me where to find the toilet tissue and I'll replace the empty roll in the bathroom."

Q. When I invite guests to dinner who have not been to my apartment before, should I give them a tour and point out where the bathroom is, etc.?
A. You needn't give a tour unless you wish to, although it is always courteous to indicate the bath-room, especially if it is not easily found.

Q. At a dinner party, should I be seated when dinner is announced, or wait for the hostess to sit down first?
A. Women may be seated immediately. Men assist the woman to their right and, if the hostess is also being seated, hesitate momentarily until she is. If the host-ess is in the kitchen or not quite ready to be seated, then everyone sits down before her.

Q. When a guest arrives late and we're already fin-ished with the first course, is that course served to the late-arriving guest?
A. No, the latecomer is served whatever course is being eaten at the time he or she arrives, unless the course is dessert, in which case he or she would be served the entrée while others have their dessert.

Q. May I ask for a second helping at a dinner party?
A. You may not ask at a formal dinner, but you may at an informal one. At a formal dinner second helpings should be offered; the hostess rings for the server when she notices that guests are ready for another portion, saying, "Would you please pass the meat and rice again?" If there are no helpers and the host has served the entrée from a sideboard, he or the hostess will usually urge guests to pass their plates to him for a second helping. To do this, leave the silver on the plate, making sure it is not right on the edge. Never hold your flatware in your hand or put it on the tablecloth when you pass your plate.

As a courtesy when only one person takes a second helping, a considerate hostess will take a little too so that her guest will not feel selfconscious or feel that she is responsible for holding everyone up.

Q. Is it appropriate to offer a toast to our hosts at a dinner party, or should they be the ones to propose a toast first?
A. As hosts, it is their prerogative to offer a toast first, although if none is offered you may certainly ask others to join you in a toast to the hosts. You may also offer a second toast if one of your hosts has offered a first.

Q. How do I indicate where people should sit at dinner if I'm not using place cards?
A. When it is time to be seated, you direct your guests by saying, "Howard, will you sit here at my left; Joan, you're here;" etc.

Q. Should couples be seated together at a dinner party?

A. Customarily, couples are not seated together. The thinking behind this guideline is that people will enjoy conversations with those with whom they do not speak daily and a livelier dinner conversation will ensue.

Q. Is it courteous to ask a guest to say grace, or is it better to say it myself?

A. It is courteous to ask, but you should ask before everyone is assembled around the table. This gives your guest the chance to refuse if she would be uncomfortable saying grace, without appearing rude by refusing in front of the other guests. When a minister or rabbi is among your dinner guests, he or she should always be asked to say grace.

Q. I am not religious. When grace is said, do I need to participate?

A. No, but you should sit quietly during grace. The same is true for those of different religions. No one should feel forced to recite a group grace or even say "amen" if it is not a part of his religious background to do so. It is only polite, however, to respect the beliefs of the others at the table and not give notice that you don't believe or that you are not participating.

Q. What is appropriate dinner music?

A. Background music during dinner should be unobtrusive, usually instrumental rather than vocal, and at a tempo that does not make guests feel rushed. It should be at a background level, not loud, so that it does not interfere with quiet conversation. Good choices include piano arrangements and classical recordings performed by ensemble groups rather than full orchestras. It should also be of a duration that does not require you to jump up and down frequently through dinner to repeat or change the tape, record or CD.

Q. We usually serve wine with dinner. Is it all right to put the wine bottle on the table or should it be poured into a decanter first?
A. If the wine bottle is not a jug, it may be put right on the table. At a larger party, a bottle at both ends of the table is most convenient. At informal dinners both red and white wine bottles may be placed on the table on saucers or in wine bottle holders. At more formal dinners red wine is usually decanted and served in the decanter.

Q. As host, how do I serve wine at the table?
A. You would serve your guests in a counterclockwise direction, beginning with the person at your right and finishing with yourself. After the first glasses of wine have been finished, you might ask someone at the other end of the table to refill glasses at that end while you would refill the glasses of those seated closer to you.

Q. *We have one friend who frequently refills his own wine glass, but never offers more to guests. Is it impolite to ask for more wine if it isn't offered?*

A. Naturally, you would prefer that he fulfill his responsibilities as host and offer you more wine, but since he seems not to realize his obligations, you would not be remiss in saying, "Mike, while you're pouring, could I please have a little more, too?"

Q. *Several times, when my family is just about to begin dinner, friends have dropped in. Should we abandon dinner to entertain them?*

A. No, you should not. Invite them in, explaining that you are in the middle of dinner and asking them to excuse you for a few minutes. Seat them in another room, provide a beverage and say that you will join them as soon as you finish dinner. If you wish, you can ask them to join you at the table, but unless your dinner is plentiful enough to share, you need only offer them something to drink while they keep you company.

Q. *When people drop in for a visit and I have something I have to get done, what should I do?*

A. You have to tell them how glad you are to see them but that they couldn't have arrived at a worse time because you are rushing to meet a deadline or to pick up your children or whatever. Then and there, make a date for them to come back for a visit.

Q. *How do I handle a neighbor who "pops by" several*

mornings a week for coffee? I enjoy her company but can't really afford the time to just sit and talk that often. She knows I'm home, so I can't pretend I'm not.

A. The next time she drops in, say, "Mary, I so love our morning coffee together, but I'm starting to fall behind in my work because I'd much rather talk to you. I don't want to give up our time together, though, so how about if we set aside an hour on Monday mornings just for us, when we're both free?" This lets her know that you are not rejecting her company yet gives specific guidelines as to what her expectations can be. If you then have other planned activities for the day you have selected, you can simply call her and tell her, changing it to another day that week or saying that you'll see her the following Monday.

Q. *What can be done about guests who won't go home?*

A. You must say, with a smile, "I'm going to have to kick you out in about 15 minutes because. . . I promised Jason I'd help him study for his history test. . . John has to catch a six A.M. flight tomorrow morning and he's got to get to bed. . . we're expected at my mom's at five and everybody still has to shower. . . it's way past time for me to feed this crowd and get them off to bed. . . " etc. Your explanation asks for their understanding, and your 15-minute warning gives them the chance to finish a drink or a conversation and then depart as though it were their idea in the first place.

Q. *Breakfast is not my favorite meal, but I seem to be invited to a lot of breakfast meetings. Does it make my host uncomfortable if I just have coffee and he wants to have a full breakfast, or is this all right?*

A. It is all right, but you might consider ordering fruit or an English muffin, which you may nibble very slowly, along with your coffee, while he is eating, to make him feel more comfortable.

Q. *Is it necessary to write a thank-you note after being at someone's home for dinner?*

A. Although it is not obligatory, either a follow-up telephone call or a thank-you note is always appreciated. In either, you should mention something unique about the evening, whether the meal, the conversation or your hosts' graciousness, along with your thanks for a lovely evening overall.

Q. *I was at a tea recently and the hostess asked me to pour. Is this supposed to be an honor? I felt stuck sitting at the tea table while everyone else was chatting elsewhere and eating and having tea.*

A. Yes, this is considered an honor. Society pages of yesteryear often noted, "And Mrs. Frederick Abercrombie poured," as part of the coverage of a tea party. Asking a guest to pour frees the hostess to see to other details. Usually, the hostess asks another friend to take over after a period of time so the person pouring can enjoy the refreshments and the company away from the tea table.

Q. *Several times when I have had buffet luncheons, some of the guests have actually pulled chairs up to the buffet table and sat there! How can I get them to move, since they are then in the way of anyone else going through the line, without seeming rude?*

A. You say, "Georgia, let me take your plate into the living room for you—I'm afraid you're going to get bumped and spilled on here and I would hate to see anything spill on that pretty dress." This phrasing implies that she has done nothing wrong, but that others might be so rude as to be in her way.

Q. *What is the ideal time of day to host a brunch, and how long should I expect people to stay? What do I do if they stay well into the afternoon?*

A. Brunch is usually served at about noon, giving the hostess the option of serving breakfast foods, a luncheon menu or a combination of both. Guests usually stay a few hours. Other than refilling coffee cups when guests linger, the hostess is not obligated to find additional snacks or begin preparing another meal. When guests have definitely overstayed their welcome, it is perfectly all right to say, "I'm so glad you could be here and that we had some special time when everyone else left, but unfortunately I have to excuse myself now and get the children going on their homework," or, ". . . get ready for a meeting tonight," or, ". . . get everybody organized because we're expected at my parents shortly."

Q. When I am seated between two people I don't know at dinner, to which do I speak and how do I include them both in the conversation?

A. When you are seated, you must introduce yourself to both, if you haven't already met. In the past, a guest would speak to the person on his right and, when the hostess turned to speak to the person on her left, would follow suit. Rarely is a dinner that formal today and there are few who remember this rule. The rule, instead, is not to ever ignore one or the other. If one of your dinner companions is engaged in conversation with the person to his other side, then you would speak to the person on your other side. If you have had a prolonged conversation with the person on your right, you should, at the conclusion of that conversation, turn to the person at your left. At a rectangular table, it is difficult to include both in one conversation which would necessitate your swiveling your head back and forth and your companions leaning in front of or behind you to speak. At a round table, it is a little easier to engage in a general conversation with both. When dinner is over, it is thoughtful to thank each before rising for being such entertaining dinner companions.

Q. I was at a dinner party recently and suddenly felt quite ill. People around me noticed, as everyone made quite a fuss, and I feel like I ruined the party. What should I have done?

A. Should this happen again, excuse yourself to the person seated next to you, rise and go to another room, or to the bathroom. If, after a few minutes away you feel better, return to your seat and make no comment about your absence. If you were seriously unwell and in need of immediate assistance, you should signal to your spouse or your hostess and ask for help.

Q. When I am offered something I don't care for at a dinner, what should I do?
A. You should say, "No, thank you." If your host insists that you "just try" something or actually brings attention to your refusal, you can say, "Brussels sprouts just don't agree with me, but the salad looks delicious," or even, "I seem to have developed an allergic reaction to garlic [or green beans, or swordfish]," or whatever. If your host continues to fuss and offers to make you something else, you would say, "Oh, no, thank you, Jean. I'm looking forward to trying your potato casserole and salad and am perfectly content," or words to that effect.

Q. I follow strict kosher dietary laws, although most of my acquaintances don't know this. I have declined several invitations to avoid creating problems for a hostess, but am hoping there is another way to handle this so that I could be a little more social.
A. When you are truly allergic to a number of foods or when you practice a certain diet for religious, health or other reasons, you may say to your hostess, "Ann, I would love to come, but my diet is so specific that, if it is all right with you, I'll bring my own din-

ner." This lifts the burden of changing the entire menu to accommodate your needs from your hostess's shoulders and still enables you to enjoy social occasions. It may make your hostess feel as though she is not entertaining you properly, but your reassurances that the pleasure of being there is what is important to you should assuage her anxieties.

Q. *I never eat dessert, but when a hostess has obviously gone to a lot of trouble to make something special, I feel rude not to have it. What should I do?*
A. If you feel you simply cannot refuse, take only a very small portion and break it into a few smaller pieces, tasting a tiny bit so that you can compliment her on her effort.

Q. *I was recently at a buffet dinner party. When dinner was announced, no one moved, despite the hostess's attempts to encourage us to go to the buffet table. What is the correct etiquette in this case?*
A. You should neither ignore the invitation to the table nor leap to your feet and fly out as if you have been kept waiting to the point of starvation. You should rise and approach the table, taking your conversational partner with you. People are always reluctant to be the first one, but you will earn your hostess's gratitude—and that of hungry but shyer guests—if you will lead the way to the buffet table.

Q. *When dinner is announced, may I take my cocktail glass with me to the table?*

A. Unless your host says, "Please bring your drink with you," don't. She may be serving wine or a meal that she doesn't feel is complemented by a cocktail.

Q. *May I smoke at the dinner table, between courses or after dinner is over?*
A. No, you may not, unless your hostess has ashtrays on the table. Even then, since so few people smoke today, you should never smoke between courses but rather wait until dinner is over.

Q. *May I help clear the table?*
A. You may help if your hostess is a close friend or relative. If the dinner is formal, or if you are somewhat of a stranger, you should not even make the offer.

Q. *At a dinner with servants, should I speak to them?*
A. No, especially not at a formal dinner, other than to say "No, thank you" or "Yes, please." If you know the servant and have not seen him beforehand, you would greet him briefly when he was passing something to you, saying, "Good evening, Bernard. Nice to see you."

Q. *When may I return my napkin to the table after dinner is over?*
A. Only when your hostess does. At that time, you make sure your napkin is smooth, but you do not attempt to refold it.

Weekends and Longer

Q. *When guests arrive for the weekend, do I show them right to their room or have them sit and talk first?*

A. Usually, those who have been traveling appreciate an opportunity to stretch their legs and get acclimated to a new environment. After greetings are exchanged, luggage should be brought in. This is the time to say, "Let me help you with your suitcase—we'll take these things right to your room." On the way, point out the bathroom and guest towels and washcloths and say, "When you're settled in, come on down to the deck (living room, kitchen, etc.) and I'll give you a tour of the rest of the house," or ". . . and we'll have lunch," or ". . . and you can tell us about your trip," etc. This courtesy gives your guests a few minutes to themselves before they plunge into life in your household.

Q. *What kind of gift is appropriate to take when visiting someone for a weekend or longer? Do I have to take a gift, or may I purchase something while I'm visiting, as a thank-you, or send something after I've left?*

A. A thank-you gift for a longer visit, when your hosts are providing all your meals and entertainment, is generally larger than a hostess gift taken to a dinner host. You may give your gift when you arrive, or you may wait and purchase something during your visit that you think your hosts will enjoy and that perhaps matches their decor or supplements a favorite activity or hobby. You may also, using the same guidelines, send a gift immediately after your visit. Examples would be a flower vase to complement a color scheme; a water game or accessory if they have a swimming pool; a condiment dish to match or complement their serving ware; or even a tea kettle if you have noticed that they don't have one. This gift would be in addition to perhaps taking your hosts out for dinner or providing a meal while visiting.

Q. *What special things can I do to make overnight guests feel that the guestroom is "their" room for the weekend?*
A. If guests will have a bedroom of their own, a bouquet of fresh flowers, a stack of recent magazines, fresh towels and washcloths (if not hung in the bathroom), a clock, a reading lamp, extra hangers and space in the closet are all signs that you welcome your guests. The bed should be made with fresh linens, the windows shining and the floors and furniture vacuumed, dusted and perfectly clean. If there is a television in the room, a television guide of programs is a thoughtful addition. If the "guestroom" is the family room converted into a bedroom for the night but still a family room by day, then you should provide a place for suitcases and personal belongings that is convenient but not obtrusive. You should also be sure that there are curtains or shades that provide privacy, and house rules for the rest of the family that ensure that no small child, accustomed to having the family room his to use, races in on Saturday morning, perches on the foot of the bed and watches cartoons!

Q. How do I find out if my guests have things they would like to do or that they would not like to do so that I know how to plan various activities?
A. You ask, if you haven't already asked when you extended your invitation or received your response.

Q. How can I remind our guests about our plans for the weekend without sounding like an activities director?
A. It is always helpful to suggest your plans for the weekend when you issue your invitation, and then to reiterate them after your guests have arrived so that they know what is expected of them. They are, after all, on your timetable, so they will be hesitant to plan or do anything until they know what you have in mind. For example, you might say, "I mentioned to you on the phone that the Johnsons have invited us all to a cocktail party tomorrow night, so we thought we'd stay at home and barbecue tonight and can catch each other up on all our news. Tomorrow, if you still feel like it, Jan, we'll spend a few hours at the outlets while the men play tennis, and then we can all relax in the afternoon until the party and dinner at the club. Sunday will be our uninterrupted day of rest, unless there is anything special you would like to do."

Q. How do I let our guests know that we are early risers but that there is no need for them to follow our timetable?
A. One of the greatest anxieties of houseguests is that they will sleep the day away while their hosts are tip-

toeing around wishing they would get up, or that they will get up too early and awaken the entire household. It is extremely courteous for hosts to communicate the morning drill. If a formal breakfast is not on the agenda and you don't plan to set your alarm clock, it is nicest of all to take your houseguest to the kitchen and say, "Here's the orange juice, bagels are in the bread drawer here, there are waffles and cold cereal. If you get up before we do, please help yourself to anything at all that strikes your fancy—except the chocolate cake, because that's for dinner." If you are indeed early risers, say so. "We seem to get up with the birds around here, but please sleep as long as you can—we aren't going anywhere until afternoon."

Q. *We visit friends a few times a year and always have a wonderful time, except in the morning. They sleep until all hours and we awaken quite early. We just stay in our room until we hear that they are up, but we would much rather go for a walk, go out for the newspaper or even go out for breakfast. Would this be rude?*
A. Although the general rule is akin to "When in Rome, do as the Romans do," you could say, "Rod and I have become early birds and usually walk a few miles in the morning before breakfast. Would you mind if we let ourselves out when we get up? If they indeed don't mind, which they shouldn't, you then have to confirm security arrangements—as in should you leave the door unlocked or could you have a key

to get back in so you aren't pounding on the door and waking them up anyway.

Q. *We have stayed a few times with friends who have an alarm system. They sleep hours later than we do and we would like to be able to go outside and swim in their pool. May I ask for the combination to shut off the alarm?*

A. No, you may not ask for the combination. This request would be most awkward for your friends if they practice what any security expert preaches, that one does not give a combination even to very best friends. You may say, "Bruce and I seem to rise with the sun and we'd love to be able to do laps before breakfast. Is there any way we can get out without setting off the alarm and waking the entire household?" They may simply give you the combination or decide not to set it at night. If they don't have a solution, then you'll just have to be sure you take a good book to read while you wait for your hosts to wake up.

Q. *Do I have to be present all the time when we have weekend guests, or is it all right to leave to go to the grocery store, for example, or to read in my room for a while?*

A. It's a blessing to all members of your house party to be able to have a little breathing room between conversations. Don't just disappear, however. Excuse yourself for a specific period of time so they know how long their "free" time is, check if there is anything your guests need and do whatever it is that you want to do. Of course, this quiet time for you should not be extended for more than two hours or your guests may think you are sorry you invited them and are secluding yourself to count the minutes until they leave.

Q. *When I am visiting someone for the weekend, how can I gracefully excuse myself for a while to give her and me some space?*
A. As long as you are not excusing yourself in the middle of dinner preparation or a planned activity, you will probably make your hostess very happy if you "disappear" for a while so she can regroup, take a nap or simply not feel obligated to be entertaining you for a short period of time. Just say, "Helen, all this sea air has made me sleepy—would it be all right with you if I took a short nap?" or "Jean, if you don't need me for an hour or two, I think I'll drag out my briefcase and tackle those papers I have to review," or "Sarah, that hammock looks so inviting—if nobody else has claimed it for the next hour or so, I'd love to try it out with the book I brought along to read."

Q. *How do I know whether to prepare lunch for weekend guests who are expected early in the afternoon? How do I know whether they will be staying for dinner on the day they are leaving?*
A. Clear communication is the key. When you confirm last-minute plans, say, "We'll have cold cuts and salads ready for lunch when you get here." They can

then say, "Oh, thank you, but we'll stop for lunch on the way," or "That would be wonderful, then we can drive straight through." To determine how long they plan to stay, don't ever ask, "When are you leaving?" which sounds a little churlish. Ask, instead, "How long can you stay on Sunday? We usually have dinner at three o'clock. Will you be able to have dinner with us before you go?"

Q. *I never am clear when friends invite me for the weekend exactly what that means in terms of when I am expected to arrive and when to leave. Is there some way to get them to give me a clue?*

A. If your friends have not been specific in their invitation, you should ask. Say, "When would you like us to arrive?" Often hosts are reluctant to give a departure time for fear of sounding rude, so it is up to you to say, "Would it be all right if we stayed until about three on Sunday, or is that too late for us to leave?" When you actually plan to leave depends on their response. If they say that would be fine, then you agree to that time. If they say, "We'd love to have you stay as long as you can on Sunday, but we will have to leave ourselves at about two for a reception at a neighbor's house," you would respond either that you would stay later or that you would then leave closer to one P.M. to give them time to get ready and go to their other party. If they suggest that you stay until a later hour, your response is dependent upon your wishes. If you wish to stay, you accept that offer. If you will need to leave earlier, you stick to your initial plan. In any case, you should communicate clearly about what your plans will be.

Q. *I have been invited to a weekend at a summer house. I would love to go, but am expecting some important telephone calls. Would it be all right for me to put my telephone on call forwarding so the calls will reach me?*
A. Before automatically forwarding your calls, check with your host and make sure he doesn't mind, for it is he, not you, who will be answering the telephone each time it rings. If he has no objection, try to keep your calls brief and to the point. It is discourteous to tie up someone else's telephone with lengthy conversations. If you need to make any calls while visiting, make collect calls or use a telephone credit card.

Q. *My wonderful friend who lives in the country often invites me for spring and summer weekends, a treat for me because I live in an apartment in the city. I would love more than anything to work in her garden. Would it be rude to ask if I could?*
A. It wouldn't be at all rude, as long as you offered to weed, edge borders and help. Only if she asks your advice on transplanting or placement, however, should you offer it: she might be offended if you started digging up her flowers and moving them to other spots! If she suggests that you surely don't want to spend your weekend working, assure her that it is what you want to do most in the world.

Q. *My family is frequently invited for long weekends at friends' beach houses. I feel I want to contribute to meals, or provide them in some way, so as not to be an imposition. How do I suggest this without interfering with our hosts' plans or going through an awkward attempt to give them money which I know they would refuse?*

A. Suggest that your family make dinner on Saturday night and say that you are bringing all the ingredients. Or say, "We want to take you and Jamie to brunch on Sunday—is that terrific place you took us to last year still there?"

Q. *How can I help with household chores when visiting?*

A. The most important help you can offer is to clean up after yourself. Clean the bathroom tub and sink when you use them, keep your possessions neatly organized, make your bed, hang up your clothes, carry used glasses to the kitchen, empty ashtrays when you fill them and refold the newspaper and put it back neatly. In addition, you can ask, "Would it be more helpful if I read the children a bedtime story or made the salad," or, "I claim kitchen duty after dinner." By indicating specific things you could do rather than asking "What can I do to help," to which the answer is invariably, "Nothing, just relax," you make it easy for your hosts to let you help.

Under no circumstances should you dust or polish vigorously without your hostesses request that you do so—it could be taken as a reflection on her housekeeping and actually be insulting, although surely helpful!

Q. *We have been invited to a friend's summer house for the weekend. I know they have a household staff. Should we make our beds in the morning or assume the housekeeper will do it?*
A. It is always helpful to make your own bed and leave your room neat. This enables the household staff to dust, vacuum, etc., which you would not be expected to do.

Q. *We visit friends periodically who do not have a guestroom and our "room" is a sofa bed in the family room. Should we fold up the bed in the morning or leave it out?*
A. You should fold it up and return it to its function as a couch. Particularly with extra people in the house, this room is a "public" room and it is awkward if it becomes off limits because you have left it as a bedroom during the day. You should also be sure your clothes are neatly stored in your suitcases and not draped around the room and that other possessions are put away during the day.

Q. *When we leave after a weekend visit, should we take the sheets off the bed and put the bedspread back over the mattress, or just make the bed, or leave it unmade, or what?*
A. You should strip the beds and place the bedspread over the mattress cover as though you were making

the bed. Fold the sheets and pillowcases you have removed and leave them on the foot of the bed. Or, if you know where it is you may carry them to the laundry area. If there are blankets on the bed, fold them as well and leave them in a pile separate from the sheets.

Q. Very dear friends have invited us for a week's visit at their ski house. We would love to go, but are worried that the old adage about "after three days, guests, like fish, begin to smell!" How can I be sure they really want us for that long and that we aren't a burden?
A. You have to assume that they would not invite you for that duration if they didn't want you to be there. And you will be a burden only if you are difficult, moody or demanding, or behave in any other antisocial way that makes your presence less than delightful. As long as you pitch in, share work and some costs and give your friends a little breathing room so that your company is not of the 24-hour-a-day variety, you should all have a wonderful time.

Q. My husband's boss has invited us both for a weekend at his country house. I know he employs a cook and a housekeeper. Should we plan to tip them?
A. No, unless you require special services above and beyond the norm. For example, if you are on a special diet and the cook prepares dishes just for you, you should make a point of thanking her before you leave and giving her a gratuity. If the housekeeper mends

or presses a garment for you, unpacks or packs your
suitcase or provides extraordinary services, you
should leave her a gratuity and a note or word of
thanks, as well. Otherwise, your host and hostess will
compensate their staff for the extra effort demanded
when guests are present.

*Q. We are fortunate to have a swimming pool, but
unfortunate in our friends and neighbors who spend
the summer in our backyard. While we are delighted
to have so many people enjoy the pool, we are not
delighted at the expectations they have that we will
continually provide refreshments, towels and even
life-guarding duties. How can we get out of this problem?*

A. Obviously you have extended hospitality to
enough people over a period of time that they feel
comfortable dropping in or dropping off their children to use your pool. Under the circumstances, the
direct approach is the most effective, and you are well
within your rights as well as all the guidelines of etiquette, to use it. Establish specific times when neighborhood friends may swim. State that children must
be accompanied by a parent because you often are
busy in the house and can't be responsible for their
safety. Stop serving refreshments and providing towels. If you wish to be more indirect, you can graciously say, when someone asks for a drink, "I'm
afraid that we are all out of soda (lemonade, iced tea,
etc.) today. Maybe next week you could bring iced
tea to share," or "...for your family." You can also

say, "I'm sorry but we don't have a clean towel left in the house—perhaps you'd better run home and get yours." If your neighbors are so obtuse that they don't respond to these gentle hints, then you must say that you can no longer provide refreshments and clean towels for everyone and they must bring their own in the future.

Q. *We recently spent a weekend at the home of an acquaintance who has a swimming pool. He never swam, even though we sat by the pool and talked, and we were dying for a swim. We felt we would be rude to just jump in. Could we have asked if we could swim?*

A. It is unfortunate that your host did not have the good sense to invite you to dive in. Even if he is not a swimmer, his hospitality should include the courtesy of offering you the privilege. If you are invited and visit again, of course, ask. You needn't mention his staying out of the water—just say, "Ben, we would love to try your pool—is it all right with you if we do?" Very likely, he is so used to having it there that he doesn't realize what a treat it is for guests to have a pool to themselves. Everyone I know who has a pool takes great delight in seeing it used, but often forget to say that while they aren't in the mood, they hope you will avail yourself of it.

Q. *We are fortunate to have a ski house and love to share our good fortune with friends. However, we don't know how far our hospitality has to go. If we*

*invite weekend guests, should we be paying for their
equipment rental and lift ticket?*
A. No, but you should make the associated costs very
clear in your invitation so your guests can decide
before they accept if they can afford the visit. Say, "If
you aren't bringing skis and boots, the ski shop at the
mountain has reasonable rentals—it's about $30 for
the weekend. And the lift ticket is $40 per person."
Naturally, if you plan to pay all the expenses, you
would not tell them the costs but you would purchase their lift tickets and arrange for their equipment
rental ahead of time.

*Q. Some friends just bought a ski house and have
mentioned several times that they will invite us for a
weekend. We're on a pretty limited budget. How can
we find out what the costs are without actually saying,
"How much will it cost?"*
A. You can't. If you don't want to ask you could,
instead, call the mountain and ask or check with a
travel agent.

*Q. When we are invited to weekend homes where
there is equipment, such as jet skis and snowmobiles, is
it correct to ask if we may use it?*
A. No, it really isn't. Think of any kind of equipment
as you would think of your host's car. It is unlikely
that you would ask him for his keys so you could
take it for a spin. In the same way, you can't, unless
offered, ask for the keys to the snowmobile or the
power boat. When a host says, "Please feel free to use

the snowmobile," it's a different story. In this case, you would say, "Tim, if it's still all right with you, I'd love to try the snowmobile—show me how to use it!"

Q. Recently, a weekend guest broke a fairly expensive tabletop. He didn't offer to replace it. May I send him a bill?
A. No, you may not. His manners are obviously terrible in that he didn't ask for the bill, but you can't remind him of his responsibility in this way. Accidents do happen and breakage is the cost of entertaining when guests are inconsiderate.

Q. My guest broke a plate from my china set. He felt terrible and insisted on paying to replace it, but I feel awkward actually sending him a bill. What should I do?
A. If you feel you cannot bill him for a replacement plate, then do and say nothing. If he is kind enough to persist, then you should feel comfortable saying, "I did replace the plate, Don—it came to $75 at Tiffany," or wherever.

Q. When visiting a friend's parents for the weekend, my son accidentally threw a baseball through their front window. He called me and told me, but they haven't said a word. Of course, I want to pay to have it replaced, but I can't find out how much the bill is. What should I do?
A. If you have discussed this with them and indicated your desire to pay for the damage and they have said,

"never mind," then you would have to investigate the approximate price of the work and send them a check with a note, "Since you wouldn't tell me the cost of the window, I've had to guess. I hope the enclosed covers it, but if it doesn't, please tell me. Kevin feels terrible about breaking the window and will give me no peace until he is sure that we have made full restitution."

Q. When visiting a friend, I dropped a glass dessert bowl by accident. I have tried to find one like it but cannot, and without it she no longer has a complete set. Should I buy her a whole new set so that all the bowls match?
A. That would be lovely, although I am sure she would not expect you to do so. Your profuse apologies and her assurances that accidents happen should conclude any further discussion on the matter.

Q. How can I tell friends that I would prefer that they not smoke in the house?
A. If your friends are serious smokers, you should let them know when you invite them that you have established a no smoking policy indoors, although they are welcome to smoke in the yard any time they would like. If they think this will be a hardship, they will have to decline your invitation to visit.

Q. Where should I put towels and washcloths for guests so that they know they are theirs?
A. If there are towel racks in the bathroom, you may

hang them there, being sure to say, "Mary, these are your towels," when showing your guest around. If there are no towel racks to spare, then you would put towels and washcloths, folded neatly on the guest beds or on a towel rack in the guest room.

Q. When there are no towels in sight, is it all right to ask my hostess for a towel and washcloth?
A. Of course, it is. Just say, "Beth, may I have a towel and washcloth? I didn't want to open your linen closet without asking."

Q. When all the towel racks are filled with family towels, what is a guest supposed to do with her wet towel after a shower?
A. You may fold it loosely and leave it on the edge of the sink or bathtub, or you may hang it, open, over the shower rail. Under no circumstances should you hang it over the back of a wooden chair in your room, or leave it on any other wooden furniture, on the bed or on the floor of your room or the bathroom.

Q. One of the hardest things about visiting in someone else's house is knowing whether I can fix myself a soda or even get a glass out of the cupboard for a glass of water. What are the guidelines?
A. As with most quandaries having to do with visiting, the best guideline is to ask. "Molly, I'd love a glass of water—may I help myself?" Aside from asking, you really cannot forage through cupboards or

the refrigerator unless you have been told you may. The thoughtful host and hostess are sure to say, "Please make yourselves at home. Sodas are here, glasses are in this cabinet, sandwich makings are on this shelf," etc. If they do not do this, a glass of water is about all you can help yourself to without discussion.

Q. *My next-door neighbor's daughter is getting married and is expecting several out-of-town guests. We have offered accommodations for a few of them. What are our responsibilities as hosts?*

A. To assist in your planning, just talk to your neighbor and find out what meals they are providing, what the timetable is and what you should plan to provide. For example, it may be that there are a variety of luncheons and dinners scheduled for out-of-town guests, but not breakfast. If they aren't inviting everyone who is staying elsewhere for breakfast, you would expect to provide this meal and should say so immediately: "I understand from Judy that the first event of the day tomorrow is a luncheon at the club, so please plan to have breakfast with us in the morning." If you don't say this, they may feel they should find the nearest diner when they get up, or simply go hungry until the luncheon. It is also courteous to point out where beverages are located and how guests may help themselves. If you are not participating in all the festivities, you would want to consider giving them a house key so you don't have to wait up for them, and you would provide bed linen, towels, washcloths and instructions on such things as television, where the iron is and where they should park so they don't block your cars in the driveway.

Q. *We are staying with some friends of my sister's during the weekend of my niece's wedding. We don't know these people at all. Are we to take them a hostess gift? How can we be their guests without intruding?*
A. Yes, you should take a small gift as a thank-you, although your sister should give a larger gift since the courtesy is actually being extended to her. You can be their guests without intruding by keeping your rooms neat, by letting them know your exact schedule and by making as little noise as possible when you are coming and going, particularly in the evening. Be sure to ask about such things as security—locking doors, opening windows, etc., and showers—ask when it would be a convenient time for you to shower so as not to intrude on the household schedule. You should be polite and courteous and, of course, engage in conversation without tying up all of your hosts' time. It is always awkward to know how much time to spend with them since they are not your friends. It is best to assume that their hospitality is mostly that of lodging, thus making everyone more comfortable about your spending quiet time in your room reading or resting rather than feeling you must seek out your hostess and spend time with her. After you return to your own home, you should write your hostess a thank-you note for her hospitality and kindness.

Q. *I love my mother, but when she visits us every summer she tends to take over, offer plentiful advice and contradict my wishes for my children. I know she is my guest, but she is also my mother, and I resent her actions sometimes. Do I have the right to tell her so?*
A. Yes, you do, but I would hope you would do so in a gentle and nonaccusatory way. Unless she is truly wrecking havoc in your household with her interference, you might try taking several deep breaths and reminding yourself that she is a guest, albeit a difficult one. It is unlikely that anything she is doing contrary to your wishes will have a lasting effect on either you or your children, as trying as it may be during her visit. She, on the other hand, would serve herself well if she remembered that she is your guest and that house rules stand, not guests' rules.

Q. *When I am visiting and need to use the telephone, should I offer to pay for my calls, and if so, how?*
A. Yes, you should. The best way to make calls from someone else's home is with a credit card. If you don't have a telephone credit card, then you should make operator-assisted calls requesting time and charges at the completion of each call. Add up what you owe, include tax and give the money, in an envelope, to your hosts. This is the case whether your host is family or friend.

Q. *I recently spent a weekend with a friend and received two work-related facsimile transmissions over his fax machine. Should I have left money for this?*

A. No, since the cost of the fax is charged to the sender. If you received pages and pages of transmissions, however, you should have left money for the fax paper, which is not inexpensive, that was used for your transmissions. If you also sent fax transmissions, you should have requested time and charges from the operator and left money for that expense.

Q. *If I have taken a hostess gift and thanked my hosts profusely for a long visit at their house, do I still need to send a thank-you note?*

A. Of course! Think how you would feel if guests came for a weekend, thanked you as they departed and then you didn't hear from them again for months. Then think how you would feel, as you were recuperating from the visit, if you got an immediate telephone call or a thank-you note in a few days that recounted some of the highlights of the visit and indicated how appreciative your guests were of your efforts and the wonderful time they had. You would feel gratified and pleased to receive the thank-you. You would feel a little disappointed to not hear a word. Apply those feelings to *your* hosts and thank them again, without fail, for all they did to make your visit so pleasant.

Q. *We were weekend guests at the home of some friends, and one of their neighbors had a dinner party to which we were invited. Should we have taken a hostess gift?*

A. No, you should not have taken a gift, but you

should have written a thank-you note when you returned home. Make sure you have the names and correct address of your dinner hosts before you leave and send them a note thanking them for including you in such a lovely evening.

Out and About

Q. *Who should follow the maitre d' in a restaurant? The host or the guest?*

A. Generally, a woman follows the maitre d' and is seated by him. This would be the case whether the woman was the host or the guest. When two women are dining together and one is hosting the other, the guest would follow the maitre d'. When they are sharing the bill, it makes no particular difference unless one is older than the other, in which case the younger would defer to the older. When a host is entertaining a group, he or she might go first so as to be able to suggest where people should sit. If he or she brings up the rear, everyone must wait to be seated.

Q. *We often entertain at our club, but seem to always have confusion when people arrive at the table as to who should sit where. Is there a more graceful way to handle this?*

A. The best way to handle this is to have a seating plan in mind and follow the maitre d' so that you can suggest seating to your guests. Having thought this through ahead of time, you don't have to count out "male, female, male," etc. to achieve balance, or make people move once seated because they are next to a spouse or in the wrong place. The men would then hold the chairs for the women to their right.

Q. *When I have invited a guest for an evening out and she insists on picking up the check, what should I do?*

A. You should be firm and say, "Thank you so much,

Jen, but this is my party. You can treat me some other time."

Q. *When I take a guest to a movie theater, should I ask her to wait in line while I buy the tickets or come with me to the ticket office?*
A. Practicality supersedes gallantry in the case of movie lines, which seem to be increasingly long. You would ask her to wait in line to ensure you have a chance at better seats while you go to the ticket window.

Q. *I prefer to entertain in restaurants but find that my guests are often uncertain about what to order. How can I let them know that they should order anything they want?*
A. Sometimes guests worry about ordering too expensive an item, or that they will be the only one ordering an appetizer or soup. It is incumbent on the host to put everyone at ease by saying things like, "The chilled shrimp are the best I've ever had, and the Caesar's salad is a must if you're a fan. . . and I can also recommend the steak au poivre," (or whatever item is at the top price range). This indicates to guests, without your having to say, "Please order an appetizer," that you expect them to do so, and that they don't have to seek out the least expensive entrée item, either.

Q. *My lunch guests sometimes insist on paying the tip. How should I handle this? If they do leave the tip and it isn't enough, what should I do?*

A. When a guest says, "I'll leave the tip," you say, "Oh, thank you so much, but I've already figured it in and it's all taken care of." If they simply take out money and put it on the table saying, "I'm taking care of the tip," you would say words to the effect of, "Thanks, Jim, but I've already got it covered. The service was pretty good, but not good enough for two tips!" He has no choice but to retrieve his money.

Q. *I have a subscription to the ballet. There are refreshments during intermissions. When I take a guest, should I also offer him something to drink between acts?*
A. Certainly, if you are planning on having a drink, you would ask him what he would like and order it for him. If he insists that the drinks are on him, there is no reason to refuse his offer, if you don't wish to.

Q. *Who should enter a row first at the theater, I as host, or my guest?*
A. The answer to your question depends on where you will end up after you enter the row. A host always gives the best seat to his or her guest, so you would go first if that would ensure that he or she would have the seat closest to the center; you would indicate that he or she should precede you if you are entering a row and walking toward the center.

Q. *What are the guidelines for traveling on someone's private plane?*
A. The basic tenets are courtesy, thoughtfulness and

neatness. Unless the private plane is very large and the staff includes a flight attendant, you are expected to locate any meals that have been brought on board, serve yourself and clean up after yourself. You should not litter nor should you expect anyone to carry your bag for you or wait on you. Naturally, you follow instructions pertaining to safety, using your seat belt when instructed to do so and remaining in your seat during takeoff and landing. Equally important is to be on time. The crew is responsible for clearing flight time, and your delay can cost them hours while they wait for a second clearance, given after preference to airlines. If you are detained for any reason, you should appreciate the value of their time and call ahead to say so, giving the time you expect to arrive.

Q. *We live near a lake and have several friends with sailboats who have asked us to sail with them. We aren't sure what would be expected of us, since we aren't sailors. What should we say?*
A. You say just that. "Ken, I'd love to come on your boat, but I don't know the first thing about sailing, so if you need a crew with experience, you'd better leave me on shore!" If your services as a crew member are not required and you have other questions, like what to wear or what kind of shoes are preferred, ask them. People love to introduce newcomers to their favorite avocations and would appreciate your forthrightness.

Q. *How do I know whether to dress for dinner when invited on someone's yacht for a short cruise?*

A. One hopes your host would indicate that dinners will be black tie or informal or semiformal or whatever, but if he doesn't, you must ask. You can simply say, "Tom, you'd best tell me the level of formality you observe on board so I don't bring my tuxedo and leave my swimsuit at home or vice versa." That is easier said to a friend. When the invitation is extended by an acquaintance, you still need to ask what kind of clothing you should pack. You could ask, "Will I need clothes other than my swimsuit and casual clothes?"

Q. When sharing a taxi with a friend and getting out at a destination before hers, do I give her half the fare plus half the tip at that point, or more?
A. You would give her half the fare plus half the tip up to that point. You are not obligated to guess what the full fare would be to her destination nor to subsidize it.

Q. I am part of a car pool and the driver is always late. Since it is his car and he is doing me a favor (although I pay my share of gas and tolls), I am hesitant to complain, but it really is a problem. What should I do?
A. You have to complain, nicely. Blame your boss or colleagues or whomever, by saying, "Frank, I'm starting to get heat at work about always being late—is there any way we could start out a little earlier?" If he says yes and still is late, then you have to say, "Frank, I really appreciate riding with you, but I'm

afraid we're just on different schedules. I've got to get in earlier than you do, and I don't want to keep putting pressure on you to start sooner—so I'm going to have to join another car pool [take the bus; take the train]," etc. "I'll miss our mornings together, but I've got no choice as long as I have this job." This enables you to part on friendly terms and leaves no residue of angry words or hurt feelings.

Q. *My wife and I enjoy cruises, but are never sure what our obligations may be at certain times. When we are having a cocktail before dinner, for example, and some people we have met join us, should we charge their drinks on our bill?*
A. You certainly may extend this hospitality, but it can establish a tricky precedent that ties you to these people night after night, taking turns buying each other drinks, for surely they would want to reciprocate the next evening or for the next round if you are having more than one drink. If you feel that you would like to buy them a drink, you should do so once. If they seem to expect that you continue to do this, your best defense is to forgo cocktails one evening or even to suggest that while this round is on you, the next round will be his. It seems unfortunate to have to remind someone else of a social responsibility, but no one today can afford to subsidize a sponge that has no intention of paying his own way!

Q. *When someone invites us to the theater, should we then insist on paying for dinner?*

A. If dinner was not part of the initial invitation, you, as guests, cannot suddenly add new dimensions to the evening by even suggesting dinner. If, however, the invitation is for dinner and the theater, you may certainly accept suggesting that dinner is your treat. If your hosts refuse this offer, be sure to reciprocate with an invitation of your own.

Q. *I have just started seeing someone who has taken me out to lunch and dinner several times. I am uncomfortable that he is spending all this money on me and would like to pay my way or take him sometimes. How do I handle this?*
A. Simple—the next time he asks you out for a meal, just say, "I'd love to, but only on the condition that this time it's my treat."

Q. *We have been invited to a friend's club for dinner. How do I know what to wear?*
A. You can ask. Say, when responding to the invitation, "We'd love to have dinner with you and are looking forward to seeing the yacht club. What's the dress code for the evening?" If you just can't bring yourself to ask, then call the club office and ask whether the dining room requires ties and jackets for men.

Q. *When we invite people for dinner at our club, is it presumptuous to tell them what to wear?*
A. If by "tell them what to wear" you mean saying that jackets and ties are required for men, or mention-

ing that you are wearing a silk two-piece dress and heels, then no, it is not presumptuous. Both these statements are very helpful to guests who may not be aware of the customary standard for dress at your club. Your guests would be embarrassed if they appeared dressed up when you were planning dinner at the poolside grill or if they showed up in casual clothing, when your reservations are for the dining room.

Q. *Often a friend invites me and my children for an afternoon of swimming at her club. I know there is a guest fee but don't know how to offer to pay it, since everything is billed to them. Do you have any suggestions?*
A. When the invitation is issued, accept under the condition that you pay the guest fee. Say that you and the children are so grateful for the opportunity to swim, but you can't continue to accept the invitations if you can't contribute to the cost. This establishes your feelings before you ever go to the club, and avoids the awkward moment of your trying to thrust money at your friend and her kindly refusing to accept it. Guest fees are usually posted somewhere near the entrance to the pool area. If the fees are not payable in cash at the gate, check the amount on the poster, put the money in an envelope and give it to your friend with your sincere thanks for a wonderful day.

Q. *When friends take us to dinner at a restaurant, do we need to return the invitation in kind or may we host them in another way?*

A. You may return the invitation in a variety of other ways. It may be that they find it easier to entertain outside their home than at home. If you prefer a comfortable evening at home, that would be the invitation you would issue. What is important is that you return the invitation within a reasonable period of time.

Q. *We were invited to an evening of bridge at someone's home. We had met this couple at another party and were pleased to accept their invitation, but haven't the time to foster a greater friendship with them. Do we have to return the invitation?*
A. Yes, you should return the invitation. Since they invited you to a party, you might include them on your guest list the next time you have a large gathering. We all run out of time these days, and unfortunately what many give up is the nurturing of new friendships. Etiquette does call for an accepted invitation to be returned, however, so you should not let too much time go by before you include this couple in an invitation of your own.

Q. *When friends suggest that we all go to the movies together, how do we avoid having them pay for our tickets or ending up paying for theirs? This has happened several times, and then the other couple feels obligated to buy refreshments. It would be so much easier if we just all paid our own way.*
A. By far the best solution is to discuss all this when you are making your plans: agree that each couple is paying their own way. Say, "Let's agree before we go

that we buy our tickets and you buy yours so that we don't have our usual money fight at the ticket window." If you do this and the other couple still try to buy your tickets, be firm in insisting that they take your money and use it to buy themselves popcorn, or whatever.

Q. *We have friends who have children the same ages as our children. Our children are all friends, as well. A few times, when we have gone out together, my friend has suggested that we share a baby-sitter. This is great, because it makes an evening out more affordable, but when they are all at my house, she just hands me money and it is never enough to cover the price of the sitter. Should I just accept this?*

A. I don't see why you should. The next time it is your house and your sitter, figure out, on the way home, how much you owe, add a tip, if you generally do, and divide the amount in half. Before you enter the house say, "Okay, Stacey's bill will come to $20, so you owe me $10." This is also kinder on Stacey than to have this discussion in front of her.

Q. *When we are going out to dinner with friends, is there an etiquette guideline about whose car we take or whether we should each drive our own car?*

A. I am an advocate of preserving the environment and participating in car pools whenever possible. If you all live close to one another and forming a car pool makes sense, it would be the host couple, if the expenses are not being split, who would drive. However, if your car is roomier or more comfortable, you could certainly offer to drive. If you live some distance from one another and are coming from different directions to meet at a restaurant, it makes better sense to drive your own cars.

Q. *When I am driving another couple for an evening out, does it matter who sits in what seat?*
A. Usually couples sit together, but if one member of the party has extraordinarily long legs or a disability that would make it more comfortable for him or her to sit in the front seat where there may be more leg room, it is a courtesy to seat him or her there.

Q. *Is there a polite way not to extend an evening when we are being driven by another couple? I always feel that I should invite them in for coffee or a drink after they have driven me home, but I seldom really want to because the hour is late and I am ready for some alone time.*
A. When you are nearing your house, begin with your thank-you's. When the car stops in front of your house or apartment building, conclude with another thank-you, and wish the driver and any other passengers a cheerful "good-night." You needn't apologize for not inviting them in nor make any comment at all about how you wish you could but you are just too tired, or whatever. Be cordial, thankful and final in your wishes for a good evening and go inside. Do not linger or talk through the car window. If you are going to stand and talk, after all, you might

as well invite them in so everyone can be more comfortable.

Q. *A friend who has season baseball tickets was unable to attend a game because he was going out of town and gave me his tickets. How do I thank him?*
A. You call him the next day and tell him what a wonderful time you had, describing a great play or some event that he would enjoy. If you can't reach him by telephone, send him a note immediately, thanking him for his generosity and telling him how much you enjoyed the game. You needn't send him a gift, but if you wish, you could buy a souvenir from one of the gift stands at the ballpark and send it to him with your note, or invite him to lunch in the near future, as a thank-you.

Q. *How do I know if someone is inviting me as a guest to a concert or asking me if I want to pay for tickets when he says, "Such and such a group is performing at the concert hall on July 16th; we're planning to go and I wondered if you would like me to get tickets for you?"*
A. This is a typically ambiguous kind of invitation, but I think you would assume that he is expecting you to pay for your tickets, if you wish to go. If you are interested, you would say, "We'd love to go with you—tell me how much the tickets are and I'll send you a check tomorrow." If he replies that he wants you to be his guests, you can either accept with pleasure or insist on sending a check.

Q. We are going on our first cruise and several friends want to come to the ship and see us off. How do we serve as hosts to them while they are there?

A. A send-off from friends and a bon voyage party is a happy way to start your trip. There are two ways of giving such a party. If you have a large stateroom, your steward will bring mixers and soft drinks, hors d'oeuvres, ice and glasses to your cabin. Often one of the guests will bring a bottle of champagne or liquor as a going-away present. If you are in a small room, you may have your party instead in one of the bars or lounges. In either case, you board the ship as early as possible and make the arrangements with your cabin steward or with the headwaiter in whichever public room you choose. This can sometimes be done before the start of the cruise. And your travel agent can take care of it for you.

Q. What does it mean to be invited to sit at the captain's table on ship?

A. It is an honor to be invited to sit at the captain's table, and the passenger so honored should not refuse without a valid reason. For this dinner, the captain is your host and you are not seated until the captain appears unless the captain sends word for his party to go ahead without him.

Parties and Special Events

❧

Q. How do I know whether or not to take a hostess gift to a party?

A. Different areas of the country and different ethnic groups have varying customs, so there is no finite rule of thumb. It is standard to take a hostess gift to a small luncheon or dinner party and to such gatherings as an evening of bridge. It is not usual to take a gift to a large cocktail party or to a party or reception held in someone else's honor and never to a formal dinner party. Host or hostess gifts are not given when you are being taken out to dinner and meeting your hosts at the restaurant, nor when you are invited to be the guests of someone at a function outside their home. You may send flowers or a gift afterward, as a thank-you, in addition to a thank-you note.

Q. When friends invite us to large parties where we don't know very many people, is it correct to introduce ourselves to others, or must we wait for our hosts to introduce us?

A. It is more than correct to introduce yourselves to others. Otherwise, you could find yourselves standing alone until someone else had the courtesy to say hello first. You would say, "Hello, I'm Harriet Sessa, and this is my husband, Vito." You would never say, "I'm *Mrs.* Sessa," unless speaking to a child. If the persons to whom you have introduced yourselves don't think to tell you their names, you should ask. Your conversation naturally will be a general one, but you may ask a specific question, such as, "Do you live here in Sacramento?" to try to initiate a conversation.

Q. Must I go through the receiving line at a reception when I don't even know any of the people in it?
A. Yes, you must. This is your opportunity to greet your hosts, to meet a guest of honor, to extend your best wishes to a bride and groom or to express your pleasure at being in attendance. A receiving line also gives your hosts the opportunity to speak, albeit briefly, with you at least once.

Q. Our hall closet isn't big enough for guest coats when we have a party. Should I take their coats and put them in a bedroom, or is it all right to direct them to the room instead so I can remain at the door?
A. If you are quite busy at the door and have no one to help with coats, then you may direct guests down the hall or upstairs or wherever you are asking them to leave their wraps. If you follow this course, you then say, "And the bar is on the terrace. Please get a drink and we'll be along shortly."

Q. What should I do when an invited guest arrives with her poodle in arms and I don't wish to have him in my house?
A. In the first place, it is extremely rude to appear on someone's doorstep with a pet in tow if the pet was not expected. Therefore, it is well within your rights to say, "I'm so happy to see Fifi, but unfortunately, she can't come in. Can you leave her in the car, or should I get a rope to tie her out in back?" If the guest, whom we already know is rude, insists on bringing Fifi into the house, simply claim acute aller-

gies or extreme dislike and be equally insistent. Remember, you did not invite Fifi; you therefore don't owe Fifi any hospitality at all.

Q. *We entertain frequently and have one regular guest who often drinks too much. Do we, as hosts, have a responsibility to stop him?*
A. Yes, you have both a legal and a moral responsibility to take him aside, tell him that he has had quite enough to drink and offer him a soda, a cup of coffee or another nonalcoholic beverage instead. Should he leave your house and injure or kill someone because he was driving while intoxicated, you could be held responsible for his condition. If he becomes belligerent or hostile, you should not confront him but immediately seek his wife's or someone else's assistance in removing him from your party before he hurts you, himself or someone else. And my advice would be that you not continue to invite him in the future. His presence and your anticipation of his crossing the line from sobriety to drunkenness are no positive addition to a party of any sort.

Q. *What do I do about a guest who arrives inebriated and is likely to spoil my party?*
A. You must take him aside and suggest that someone drive him home because it is obvious that he has had too much to drink and you wouldn't want him to be embarrassed the next day. If that is not possible, then you must try to direct him to a bedroom where he can rest until he feels better and is able to join the

party. An inebriated person is not one to necessarily be practicing manners himself, so you might expect belligerent or hostile behavior. If this occurs, you must be firm, and if he is particularly hostile, you may have to suggest that you will call the police if he doesn't stop his behavior and take your suggestion that he rest a while. In the meantime, try to take his car keys away from him so he *cannot* drive. This is not a time to be excruciatingly polite and worry about hurting his feelings. He is not extending that courtesy to you.

Q. How do I discourage someone who has had enough to drink from having another?
A. You tell him, point blank, that he has had enough to drink, that you are responsible for him and that, as his host, you cannot allow him to have another drink. If he becomes uncivilized in his behavior, you would do best to elicit the support of his spouse, if present, or another guest, to remove him from your party, take him home or take him to another room to sober up. You should be sure he does not have his car keys or, if he does, that they are given to a responsible person to transport him. If you let him drive in an inebriated condition and he causes an accident, you could be held responsible for his condition.

Q. Several of our friends will be guests at my son's wedding. What are my obligations to them? I don't want to seem too "hostessy" since the bride's parents are actually the hosts.

A. Your obligations are to talk with them during the cocktail hour, to be sure they are seated at a congenial table, if you are asked for input when seating plans are drawn up, and to visit their tables, if they are not seated with you, at some time during the reception.

Q. *I am in charge of the teachers recognition lunch at my daughter's school. How do I keep other parents from eating until all the teachers have been served, without seeming bossy or rude?*
A. You can't. You'll just have to remind them of their own manners. You can be light about it and say, "Ladies, we've worked so hard to show the teachers that we appreciate them—we'd better not eat any more until they've been served or they'll think we don't care after all!"

Q. *What can I do about a guest who is telling unpleasant "jokes" at a party?*
A. You can interrupt him in the middle of a joke and say, "Jerry, could you give me a hand in the other room for a minute?" Take him aside and tell him that while you've always appreciated that he has a sense of humor, there are other guests who aren't so appreciative and you would be grateful if he could refrain from telling off-color jokes because they might become uncomfortable. In this way, you aren't embarrassing him in front of the others.

Q. *What is the best way to introduce a new friend to others at a large cocktail party? Should I simply escort*

*her around the room and introduce her to everyone,
or is it all right to leave her with a few others so I can
attend to those who are still arriving?*
A. You can ask another friend if she would look after
your new friend for a few minutes while you stand
door duty. Ask your other friend to please introduce
her to those she hasn't met. If you have no one to ask
to do this, then you would take your new friend to a
group of people who are talking together, introduce
her, chat for a minute and then excuse yourself. You
would then go back and retrieve her, later, to introduce her to others.

Q. *We have been invited to a tree-trimming party at
Christmas time. Are we supposed to take something to
our hosts?*
A. The usual hostess gift for a tree-trimming party is
a small ornament for your host's tree or another holiday decorative or food item.

Q. *If everyone is having a good time, would it be rude
of the hosts to encourage their guests to remain longer?*
A. Not at all! It shows that you are enjoying their company, too, and if their offer to leave seems tentative, it is
far friendlier to say, "Oh, don't go—it's Friday night
and we can all sleep late tomorrow morning," than to
jump up and bring them their coats the minute someone says, "Well, it's getting late." If, however, they
really must leave, one suggestion that they stay is
enough. Don't force them to remain if they have a
baby-sitter waiting or are firm in their resolve to go.

Q. *Who should be in the receiving line at a reception held in someone's honor?*

A. The receiving line would consist of the host and/or hostess, the guest of honor, the guest of honor's spouse, if present, and in some cases, various officials of the committee giving the reception.

Q. *Should there be a receiving line at a tea party held in someone's honor?*

A. No, there is no receiving line, but the guest of honor and the host and hostess should stand together near the door to greet arriving guests. Once everyone has arrived, conversations are informal.

Q. *I was guest of honor at a party given for me. Was I supposed to be the first to leave, thereby releasing everyone else, or the last?*

A. You are supposed to be the first to leave. This rule is more or less obsolete, however, so if other guests must depart, they may do so before the guests of honor does.

Q. *At a recent dinner party, the hostess announced that we would play charades after dinner. I declined, since I thought this was ridiculous. My wife was furious with me and said I was rude. Was I?*

A. Yes indeed, you were. However ridiculous you thought the entertainment, if it was neither against your moral fiber nor dangerous, you should have acceded to your hostess's wishes. It was only for a short period of time, no doubt, and you were her guest. As such, it was an obligation to go along with her plans, no matter how silly you felt.

Q. *If I am having a really terrible time at a party, how soon may I leave without seeming rude?*
A. You can leave politely no sooner than an hour into the party when the party is large, a cocktail party or a reception. If it is a dinner party, you are almost obligated to stay at least through dinner, since your hostess will have set a place for you or made other accommodations for you. When you do leave very early, you should, to spare your host's feelings, plead a terrible headache or the onset of a cold rather than just walk out with no explanation at all.

Q. *How long should a guest remain at a party?*
A. Dinner guests should stay at least one hour after dinner, since it is hardly complimentary to the hostess to "eat and run." At a small party a couple should not leave long before anyone else seems ready to go, because their departure is very apt to break up the party. Otherwise, a guest should stay as long as he wishes within reason, while being sensitive to noticing if the host and hostess and others at the party begin to look tired, in which case he should say his good-byes and depart.

Q. *We recently attended a dance as the guests of some friends. My wife told me I had to dance with our hostess. Was she right?*
A. Yes, she was. When you are the guest of another couple at a dance, it is polite and expected that you

will ask your hostess to dance once during the evening. It is thoughtful if you do so when there are others still at the table so that you don't leave your wife sitting by herself. You are not obligated, however, to ask other women at the table to dance except for the woman seated next to you.

Q. *We often attend large parties. Just as often, we seem to leave before the party is over. Is it necessary to seek out our host and our hostess to thank them, or may we just go?*

A. Except in the case of very large public receptions, it is necessary to find and thank both your host and hostess. It is easier if you do this as a couple rather than wandering about separately trying to find them. You would thank them graciously for the lovely time you had and then depart. You would not bid all the other guests farewell as you depart, since your early exit might make them feel they should leave, as well.

Q. *I have been invited to several birthday and anniversary parties where the invitation read "no gifts please," yet several guests came with gifts. What is correct?*

A. It is correct to respect the indication on the invitation. If the one being honored is a very close friend, or the couple dear friends, you would give them a gift separately, at another time.

Q. *At a B.Y.O.B. party, is it acceptable to collect your bottle and take it with you when you leave?*

A. Yes, it is, although some people feel uncomfortable doing this. The concept of "Bring Your Own

Bottle" helps hosts keep their own costs down, but the expectation is not that they will have a large liquor supply at the party's end. If you find it uncomfortable to retrieve your bottle and exit with it, then don't take a full bottle with you—take just as much as you think you will drink so you are leaving little behind, or take your beverage in a personal flask which you, of course, would take with you.

Q. Are there any guidelines for stocking the bar for a cocktail party?
A. There are two tips that are especially important to pay attention to: First, be sure to have enough; and second, be sure that drinks are mixed properly. As a general rule, you should count on each guest's having at least three drinks. Since a quart of liquor will provide 21 one-and-one-half-ounce drinks, one bottle will serve approximately seven people. Even though the occasion is called a *cocktail* party, not all of your guests may choose an alcoholic beverage, so you *must* have nonalcoholic drinks available. Tomato or other fruit juices, colas, mineral water and ginger ale are all popular substitutes. It is also thoughtful to have diet sodas available. You should also have a quantity of white and red wine and beer for guests who prefer them, and a supply of cocktail condiments including lemon peel, limes, olives and cherries.

Q. Is it appropriate to hire a bartender for an at-home cocktail party?
A. Yes, particularly if you are planning a cocktail

party for more than 18 or 20 people. One bartender can serve between 20 and 30 people very well. If it is a really large party, the services of a waiter or waitress as well will make the evening much more pleasant.

Q. *Is it proper to request a song of a band when you're a guest at someone else's party?*
A. Yes, it is. It is also proper to provide a tip of a dollar or two when making the special request.

Q. *May my husband and I give ourselves an anniversary party, or does this have to be hosted by someone else?*
A. Early anniversary parties are always given by the couple themselves. By the time they reach the 25th anniversary, they may well have grown children who want to make the arrangements, but it is perfectly correct for them to do so themselves. Sometimes close friends plan a celebration, and this is appropriate, as well.

Q. *The number of invitations for my son's graduation is limited, but we would like to have a party to celebrate his achievement. Is it all right to invite people to the party who have not been invited to the graduation? How do I let them know that we aren't requesting presents, just their presence?*
A. It is fine to plan a graduation party and include as many people as are close to your family and to your son, in particular. Many people will assume that gifts are in order, but if you are concerned that your invi-

tation will be interpreted as a bid for a gift, simply write "no gifts please" at the bottom of the invitation. If some guests do bring gifts, they should not be opened at the party. If a ceremony is made of gift-opening, those who don't bring a gift will feel remiss that they didn't. Whether gifts are opened privately during the party or later, the graduate must write thank-you notes immediately.

Q. Should we have a receiving line at my daughter's graduation party?
A. No, there is not a need for a formal receiving line, but the graduate, as the guest of honor, should be near the door to greet guests so that they can congratulate her.

Q. Our baby will be baptized soon. Do we need to have a party afterward?
A. It is not at all necessary to hold a reception or party to celebrate a christening or baptism, although a small brunch or lunch with godparents and other close friends and relatives in attendance is appropriate and a nice way to extend the happiness of the day.

Q. We have recently moved and would like to invite friends to a housewarming party, but aren't sure what form this party should take. Are there any guidelines?
A. A housewarming is generally a cocktail party or a cocktail buffet. It may be as simple or as elaborate as you wish, and it always includes a tour of the house and grounds.

Q. We have been invited to a housewarming party. Should we take a gift of some kind?

A. Yes, it is customary to take a gift to a housewarming party. The gift should be something useful or decorative for the house. It needn't be large or expensive, but it should be thoughtful, fun and useful to the new residents.

Q. What, exactly, is a sweet 16 party?

A. A sweet 16 party is simply an elaborate birthday party celebrating the milestone of turning 16. This age is considered by some as the real division between childhood and young adulthood. Sweet 16 parties are always for girls—although boys do have birthday parties to celebrate attaining their 16th year, they would never be called "sweet." Parties may take any form. They may be for girls only, they may be slumber parties or they may be for both genders and include dinner and dancing. They can also be brunches, hayrides, theater parties, weekend house parties or swimming-pool parties. The importance is that the focus is on the birthday person and that a part of the party is a celebration of her birthday.

Q. If a guest spills something on my carpet during a party, is it rude to clean it up right away?

A. It is only rude if you shout at your guest, call her a clumsy idiot or twist your face into a grimace of agony. Swiftly dealing with the spill relieves both you and your guest, particularly when accompanied by the comment, "See, no damage done!"

At Business Gatherings

Q. My company has annual picnics for all employees and their families. As director of my division, do I have social responsibilities to those in my department?
A. Your prime responsibility is to greet everyone from your department who attends. You will be particularly beloved if you remember the names of spouses and even children and make a point of greeting them by name. Throughout the day, if you see that someone is alone or seems shy, try to spend an extra minute or two with him but also help him to move into a group of co-workers or other guests.

Q. Unfortunately, our office holiday party frequently gets out of hand. What should I do about people on my staff who are behaving inappropriately?
A. This can be difficult, since, although a company function, the party is more social than business in nature. If the behavior is inappropriate but not offensive, you might ignore it. If, however, you observe someone who is obviously inebriated or who is harassing others, you must step forward, call her aside and suggest that she should consider leaving the party since you know she will be sorry the next day for having offended other people and you don't want to see her further embarrass herself.

Q. When a client says, "Let's have lunch," is it expected that he is paying, that I am or that we are sharing the bill?
A. Generally, you would entertain your clients as a way of thanking them for their business. If a client

makes the suggestion, however, you would assume that she was picking up the tab. It would be preferable, of course, for her to say, "I'd like to take you to lunch. . . ."

Q. *My company's sales meetings are usually out of town over a period of several days. How far do my obligations extend, as division head, to socializing with those on my staff? Is it permissible for me to order room service, for example, on those evenings that aren't scheduled for group dinners, or am I expected to be present at all times?*

A. You are not expected to be present other than at those scheduled meetings and meals for the entire division. You surely would welcome a quiet, room-service dinner on a free evening, and should not hesitate to avail yourself of the opportunity.

Q. *My office is fairly formal in the use of titles in the office (Mr. Andrews, Miss Hellman) but several people do socialize after hours on a first-name basis. What form should be used at staff luncheons or other events outside the office that are still business functions?*

A. The same form that is used in the office would be used at business functions in restaurants, clubs or other off-premise locations.

Q. *Should business associates be invited to a family wedding or other family social occasion?*

A. Business associates who are not also close personal

friends would be invited to a family wedding only if it is acceptable to the bride or groom and if the wedding is quite large. If you choose to invite associates, be careful not to slight anyone by failure to extend an invitation to a large wedding. If you invite one, invite all with whom you work, including your boss. If the wedding is smaller and more personal, however, you need invite only those business people who also are your friends.

Weddings should never be used as an opportunity to pay back the business obligations of the bride's or groom's parents or as an excuse to promote a deal or a business relationship.

Whether business people are invited to other family social occasions depends on the same considerations. If the affair is small and intimate, you need invite only business associates who are friends. If it is large and you are inviting business associates who are only that, you again should be careful not to exclude anyone who would feel left out if not included.

Q. The head of a firm with which I do considerable business has invited me to his daughter's wedding. I am not particularly interested in establishing a social relationship. Must I attend? If I don't, must I send a gift anyway?
A. No, you needn't attend, but yes, you must send a gift. A wedding invitation demands a gift in return, regardless of whether you attend.

Q. A client has extended a social invitation to a family

gathering. I prefer to keep or relationship on a business level. Must I accept his invitation?

A. No, you need not accept. As with any personal invitation that you wish to decline, send or call your regrets explaining that you have another commitment. Keep your return invitations to the client on a strictly business lunch or dinner level. If this client persists in inviting you to more social gatherings, you may say, "Harry, I enjoy our meetings immensely, but my family just isn't able to support my business life, they are so busy themselves. They've asked that I not commit them to any more professional social gatherings, so I'll have to decline your kind invitation."

Q. My boss invites me to lunch every few months. Should I return these invitations?

A. No, you should not. Although you would return a social invitation, such as dinner at his home, you do not return a lunch invitation, leaving your lunches together to be his prerogative.

Q. When returning a social invitation to my boss, should I just ask him in the office or actually send him an invitation?

A. If you are a woman, write an invitation to your boss and his or her spouse; if you are a married man, ask your wife to write the invitation; if you're an unmarried man, write it yourself. The invitation is mailed to their home, not to the office.

Q. *My boss and her husband invited us to a restaurant for dinner. When we return the invitation, should we also take them to a restaurant?*

A. No, you need not reciprocate your boss's invitation in kind. For example, you may repay a fancy dinner at a restaurant with a simple buffet dinner in your home.

Q. *It is often difficult to schedule lunch appointments with clients. Is it acceptable to invite a client to a business dinner?*

A. Yes, it is acceptable. Dinner invitations should be extended well in advance of the date. An executive's secretary may either telephone the prospective guest or write him a note saying that Mr. Barrett would like to take Mr. Smith to dinner on the 14th. Those without secretaries make the invitations themselves in the same way. The invitation should be addressed to the business person only, at his office, so that it will be clear that spouses are not included. A reservation should be made at a convenient restaurant, at a somewhat quiet table or in a private room.

Q. *I have found it convenient to host business gatherings at my club, but I am never sure of the best way to make arrangements. Any advice?*

A. When you do this kind of entertaining, you may meet at the club in the morning, play golf or tennis, eat lunch and then part, either to return to work or to go home. You may prefer to conduct business in the office in the morning and then arrive at the club for lunch, followed by golf, tennis or swimming. Be sure to include specifics in your invitation, such as the dress code for the restaurant, the need for tennis whites, etc.

Q. I would like to invite the members of my department and their spouses or significant others to a dinner party, but I don't want the evening to turn into an extension of the office. What can I do to ensure that the conversation is more general?

A. You are being thoughtful to the spouses or escorts of your staff when you express this concern, for surely nothing can be more boring, or perhaps more political, than moving the office to your home for a social evening. You have to, when you hear business talk occurring, say, "Nancy, the office is off limits tonight—tell us instead about how that new addition to your house is going," or "George, I wanted this evening to be a break from what you do all day: Show me that picture of the new baby and tell me what wonderful things he is doing by now." This fairly gentle approach precludes your having to make a general announcement and helps your guests to relax and believe that you are genuinely interested in their lives beyond the office.

Q. My husband has his own life and his own career, yet he has always been supportive of mine. If I were to have a party for co-workers, what would his role be?

A. When you entertain colleagues at home, your husband or wife is there to support you: to make your guests feel welcome, to help them enjoy being with you both, as well as to assist with the duties of being a host couple. Since there will undoubtedly be a lot of shop talk, it is your spouse's job to be interested—to listen, to ask questions, to indicate the involvement of both of you in the company. Yet your husband or wife is an individual, too, and, as such, is interesting to your business associates. He or she should feel free to discuss his or her profession and personal concerns. . . but not too much about the family, please! In short, a spouse should act in such a way that when guests leave they are able to say, "What a nice couple!"

Q. *My wife and I have a small country house and are considering taking turns inviting business associates for a weekend. Do you think this is a good idea?*
A. It is a good idea only if you know them well. If you don't feel extremely comfortable with them, a weekend can create tension because there is no escape. It is easier if you have an option of facilities such as swimming, boating or tennis. It is also easier if you plan ahead, preparing as much of each meal in advance as possible so that you are not relegated to the kitchen for great amounts of time, thus leaving guests to their own devices and perhaps uncomfortable with nothing to do. It is also a good idea if you can plan some activities, such as a trip to a site of particular interest to the area, a country auction, a summer theater or a local fair. This gives a focus and entertainment that diverts guests from having only

one another to talk to when they aren't totally comfortable in one another's company.

Q. *Am I expected to return a business invitation in the same way that I am obligated to return a social invitation?*

A. No, you are not. Business invitations need not be returned in the same way that social invitations must be. If a salesperson invites you or if, as a client, you are entertained, you are not expected to repay this business lunch or dinner, although you certainly may if you have continuing business together. Neither are you expected to repay a social invitation where you, as a client, have been entertained, even if the invitation has included your spouse or your entire family. You are, however, expected to return social invitations from co-workers and other business associates who have extended a hand of friendship to cement a business relationship or simply because you enjoy one another's company outside the office or your business ties.

Q. *I enjoy my staff, and would like to entertain them socially, but am concerned that this may be in conflict with my role as the department head. What do you think?*

A. You are correct in that you must exert some caution in undertaking home entertaining that merges your business and social lives. As an upper management person, you may weaken your position of authority, making it difficult to reprimand or fire someone or to pass over someone for a raise or a promotion. For this reason, home entertaining of business associates should be confined to peers or to clients who have become friends, leaving the entertaining of office staff to that of an occasional home party.

Q. *Who writes a thank-you note to my boss and his wife when they have entertained us socially; would I, or would my wife?*
A. Since this was a social invitation, the thank-you note is social in nature, as well. Therefore, whichever of you normally would write a note to thank a hostess for a nice evening, a weekend or whatever, would do so in this case, as well. The note should include the name of the other person, as in, "Perry and I so enjoyed our evening with you and will never forget our first experience with escargots, thanks to your encouragement..." It should be signed with the name of the person who writes the note, not by both.

Q. *Where should a thank-you note for a social evening written to my boss be sent?*
A. If the evening was truly social and spouses were involved, or the event was an out-of-office entertainment, such as a sporting event, you would send the note to your boss's home. If his or her spouse was involved, it would be addressed to both.

Q. *My office is having a holiday party after work on Friday. What is the proper attire?*
A. At a party held in the office, both men and women

generally appear in the clothes they have worn all day. They may even have put on a somewhat fancier dress or jacket than usual that morning in anticipation of the event. Women may elect to add accessories, but overdressing would be out of place. At an office party held outside the office, both men and women may properly change from work clothes into dressier clothes, but should remember that it is a business affair and overly dressy clothing is not appropriate.

Q. The people in my office held a baby shower for me after work one day. They gave me a collective gift. How do I write a thank-you note?
A. You would write one note, with the salutation "Dear friends," thanking everyone for the shower and the gift. You would mail the note to the office manager or the boss's secretary or whoever seems to be efficient in communications, and he or she would be responsible for routing the note to everyone involved.

Q. Do I take the equivalent of a "hostess gift" when being entertained at lunch or dinner by a business associate?
A. No, you do not. Gifts are taken only for at-home business entertainments, whether dinners or weekend visits, never for business lunches or dinners.

Q. I am having a party and want to invite some people from the office who have become friends. Is this all right?
A. Yes, but be sure that the invitations are private—

mailed to home addresses—so that those not invited do not feel offended or left out. In fact, one of the nicest ways to entertain business associates is to include one or two with nonbusiness friends. This makes them feel like personal friends about whom you care enough to share your social as well as your business life.

Q. *I would like to invite some co-workers to a holiday party. I am living with someone, a fact which I haven't mentioned in the office. How should I introduce him?*
A. Your partner is treated exactly as a spouse would be and would serve as a co-host, just as a spouse would, but you don't need to give him a "handle" when introducing him. Simply say, "This is Reid Thomas." Do not add, "my boyfriend" or "my roommate" or "my lover" as means of identifying him. His identity as a person is all that is important.

Q. *My boss has invited me, along with others, to his summer house for a party to celebrate the completion of a huge project. My problem is that I don't drive and I have no way to get there. I'm not sure who all is invited, and I hate to ask someone for a ride in case she's not. What should I do?*
A. Explain your situation to your boss, along with your sensitivity to not wanting to mention the party to just anyone in case he or she is not invited, and ask him if he could tell you who else is on the guest list so that you could try to arrange transportation.

Q. *My new job involves entertaining out-of-town associates. Although I don't have any budget restrictions, I'm not sure what I should plan.*
A. You should plan a dinner for one evening of their trip, including a few from your office who will have business with the traveler. If the trip is prolonged, you should ask what the associates would like to see. If you live in an area where there is a range of theater, sports, nightclub and other entertainments from which to choose, simply ask which they would prefer, explaining that you look forward to taking them. If your area offers little in the way of entertainment, then one or two dinners with small groups from the office included are sufficient. Remember that it is tiring to travel, and it may be that the visitor would relish an early evening with room service and a movie, by himself, in his room!

Q. *Part of my job includes entertaining associates from other countries. This can be a strain when their English is not strong and I have no skills in their language. How can I make them more comfortable and entertainments more meaningful?*
A. You should not select events where language skill is integral to enjoyment, such as plays, comedy acts or English-language movies. You should look for concerts, ballets or other dance performances where language is less important. If you plan to entertain at dinner, it would be helpful to find an associate or a friend who has some proficiency in that language to help interpret and make conversation easier.

Q. I work in a fairly large office, and it has been tra-dition to celebrate such events as the birth of a baby, a birthday of an employee, an upcoming wedding, etc., in some way. It has fallen to me to plan these events, but they are getting out of hand and very expensive. Do you have any suggestions for ways to tone down the cost yet still celebrate?

A. This is a common problem, and one solved best by cooperative thinking. If collections for gifts are becoming a daily occurrence, you might discuss the possibility of collecting $10 or so from everyone in the department in January and using that pool of money to buy a small gift as occasions occur. If you literally celebrate, with an office party, you might see if a majority of the employees would like to forgo this component and just give a gift. It is possi-ble that everyone will be relieved to have a solution that removes the time and expense required to keep up with the entire office list of commemoratives. If no one is willing to take a stand, you should talk to the department head or supervisor and ask for her or his suggestions or even sanction changing the tradi-tion.

Q. Is it appropriate to celebrate a retirement with a party, or does this look as though one is glad the per-son is leaving?

A. Unless a person has been forced to retire against his or her will and he or she is bitter or unhappy, a party is most appropriate. A retirement party is not a gesture of jubilation over someone's departure, but rather a recognition of their long years of service and their desire to move on to another stage of life.

Q. *A longtime member of our staff died recently and there was an announcement that friends and family were invited back to his house after the service. My associates and I did not know if we should go or not since we didn't fall into either group. What should we do in this situation?*

A. If there were no visiting hours at the funeral home and no receiving line after the service to enable you to personally express your sympathy, then you could have stopped by for a few minutes to pay your respects, in person, to the deceased's family. You naturally would not stay for very long, but family members and close friends always appreciate the kind sentiments of co-workers and others who have known the deceased over a period of time.

Q. *When there is an office-related but social party where spouses are invited, is it appropriate for me to attend without my husband? He is not enthusiastic about going to my company's events and I frankly have more fun if I am not worrying that he is bored or unhappy about being there.*

A. It is appropriate for you to attend without your husband. When accepting the invitation, be clear that you are accepting for yourself and regretting for your husband.

Children as Guests
and Hosts

❧

Q. When my daughter invites little friends to play, they spend half their time saying, "What do you want to do?" "I don't know. What do you want to do?" How can I help her to be a good hostess?

A. Suggest that she think, in advance, about what her friend seems to like and make a mental list of four or five activities she would enjoy, too. Help her learn to say, "Would you like to play with the dollhouse now or color on the driveway with chalk?" When we offer a few choices we make it easier for our guests to respond favorably to one. When we just ask "What do you want to do?" they are unsure as to how to respond.

Q. Do you think gifts should be opened at a child's birthday party?

A. Some parents do not let their children open their gifts until everyone has gone home, partly because they want to keep all duplicates intact so they can return or exchange them. I believe that children should open their gifts in front of their friends, for several reasons. First, it is one of the moments of the party where they are in the limelight. Second, other children are often excited about the gift they are giving and are anxious to see the birthday child open it and express pleasure. Third, it is an opportunity for children to use their best manners and express their best "thank-you's."

If you are concerned about keeping gifts in their original plastic wrapping in case they need to be exchanged, be on hand to take each gift after it has been opened, passed around and examined, and put it aside so there is no temptation for party guests who would enjoy opening them right up and playing with them then and there. If asked, just say, "Next time you come over you can play with this with Billy, but he gets the first chance to open it and play with it because he's the birthday boy!"

Q. *My son is having a birthday party. I am worried that, if he opens a gift that is something he already has, he will say so, upsetting the gift-giver. How can I help him avoid doing this?*
A. It is difficult enough for an adult to think of an appropriate comment in the same situation, but your desire to help your child be prepared is admirable. Explain to him that casting a gift aside with an "I already have this" can be upsetting to his friend. Suggest, instead, that he simply say, "Thank you so much! What a great gift. If you explain to him ahead of time that this may happen and that he shouldn't worry because you will help him exchange one of them for another toy, he won't be as disappointed.

Q. *Do you have any feelings about forcing children to share, particularly with strangers? I was in the park with my children when children they did not know took their toys and started playing with them. My children were really upset, so I retrieved the toys. The mother of the other children castigated me for not teaching my children to share. Was she right?*
A. Certainly not! It is unlikely that the mother would pass over her car keys to share her car with you or

offer you half the sandwich she was eating. In the same manner, children should not expect to be able to take anything they like, just because they like it. There are times when it is necessary to share—when your children invite a friend over to play, it is understood that they will share their toys. When they are playing at nursery school and there is a toy another child wants, too, they will probably be asked by the teacher to share. But to be expected to share with strangers is unreasonable.

Q. *My daughter is generous about sharing her toys, but there are some things that are special to her. Is there a way to help her refuse to share these things when friends, who are tough on toys, are visiting?*
A. Probably not, since young children don't necessarily understand this. Instead, respect her wishes and help her put away any toys she doesn't want to share so that the issue doesn't even come up. An expensive marionette, a beautiful doll, etc. should not be sacrificed to rough-and-tumble children, but saying no sounds selfish, even though it isn't. Putting the toys out of sight saves everyone's feelings and your child's anxieties.

Q. *My daughter, who is 14, has several friends who often drop in to see her. I am delighted, but her skills as a hostess leave something to be desired and leave me in the position of having to entertain her guests— and I don't have time to entertain my own guests. How can I help her?*
A. Have a conversation with your daughter about the

friends' homes she feels the most comfortable in, and why she feels that way. See if she can identify those things that make a guest feel welcome. After she has done this, ask her what she can do to make her friends feel welcome in your home. Tell her what the limits are for refreshments and explain that you expect her to clean up after her friends. Talk about how she feels when she is left out of something, and ask her if she can think of a way to be sure that her guests do not feel left out. This is usually a more effective approach than giving her a lecture or a series of do's and don't's.

Q. *My house is pretty informal. I am going to spend a week at my roommate's parents' house. What do I need to know?*

A. That's a pretty big question, but remembering the basics of being a good guest should set you on the right course. First, you, as a young person, stand when your friend's mother enters the room for the first time. You wait for her to extend her hand to you; you do not offer to shake hands with her first. You are courteous and quiet during quiet times. You offer to help with everything from carrying grocery bags to clearing the table after dinner. You make your bed in the morning, you keep your feet and shoes off the furniture and bedspread, you do not make telephone calls without asking first and paying for them and you are kind to any siblings your friend may have, even if she isn't particularly kind to them herself. You also should keep in mind that your roommate's mother would more than likely appreciate some alone time with her daughter, so you make yourself scarce every now and then, pleading studying, a letter to write or the desire to take a walk around the block or into town. If you accomplish all these thoughtful goals, you will surely be a welcome guest again and again.

Q. *My daughter's friend is often at our house. When her mother comes to pick her up, she won't come in but stands in the doorway, usually for at least 15 minutes, talking. I invite her in but she always says she is in a hurry, yet she is delaying me from what I have to do. What can I do without being rude?*
A. You can insist that she come in for a few minutes while you finish washing the lettuce or stuffing envelopes, or whatever your project of the moment is. Say, "Janet, I'm right in the middle of sorting magazines—come keep me company while I finish." If this doesn't work, then make sure the child is ready at the time her mother usually arrives and have her at the door. The minute her mother arrives, open the door, walk the child out to her mother, exchange pleasantries and then excuse yourself because there is "something on the stove" or "someone on the telephone," etc.

Q. *I love my godchild dearly, but when she and her parents visit she stays up as late as we do. She is only seven, and as the hours go by she gets more and more demanding, making it impossible for us to have an adult conversation. Is there some polite way I can suggest that she be put to bed?*

A. Probably not, but you could try by asking, before dinner, "When is Sandy's bedtime? I don't want to serve dinner too late so that she is tired—and do want to leave time for you to be able to tuck her in before we settle down for some serious catching up!" This is a pretty broad hint that you expect your godchild to be put to bed at a reasonable hour, without causing rancor or resentment that you are trying to take charge.

Q. *My son has a friend who seemingly has an attention-deficit disorder since he is unable to focus on anything for more than a few minutes. By the end of his visits, my son is frantic. How can I help him learn to entertain this child?*

A. You have to explain to him that Kenny seems to have a problem concentrating on anything for very long. You can say that other children have that problem, too, and that you know it makes it very hard to have him over to play. Suggest a list of activities that your son could engage in with his friend, and arrange a "high sign" for him to give you when he has had enough so that you can intervene either with a snack or an announcement that play time is over. There are some situations that are just too difficult for children to handle without parental help, but talking with them about what some of the problems can be makes them feel better about their own abilities and even may spark some creative thought about ways for them to help.

Q. *My boyfriend and I are going to the prom together. He is paying for a limousine and the prom tickets, and he has invited me to the picnic and party the next day. I think he is paying for a lot and would like to pay for the day-after activities. Is this proper?*

A. It is more than proper, it is generous and thoughtful. I imagine, since you call him your boyfriend, that you are close and that suggesting this to him would not be difficult. This way, you can be each other's guests and share the costs as well as the fun.

Q. *We are planning to visit my husband's sister and family for the weekend. My children have certain television shows they like to watch. How can I be sure that they are not monopolizing the television set or that there isn't something else my niece and nephew would rather watch?*

A. If you have a VCR at home, set the timer to record the shows so your children can watch them when you return home. If not, the easiest thing is to ask your sister-in-law if it is all right if your children watch a particular show at a particular time or if that will cause a problem. If she doesn't permit that much television-watching and is rigid in her rule, even with guests in the house, then your children will have to skip their shows for the weekend. If she doesn't mind but there is a show on at the same time that your niece and nephew usually watch, it still may be that your children cannot watch their own show, although hospitality dictates that your children, as guests, should be given preference. It isn't up to you to point this out, however, so it may be a good idea to prepare your children for possible disappointment, reminding them that the purpose of the visit is to see their cousins, not to watch television.

Q. *My 11-year-old daughter is a truly picky eater. She is sometimes invited to stay at a friend's house for lunch or dinner. What guidelines can I give her so that she doesn't continually say "I don't like that!"?*
A. You have to make sure that she says, "No, thank you" when she is offered something she doesn't care for. Tell her that it is not polite to make such comments as "that is disgusting" or "I hate the way that tastes," which is of no interest to anyone else and can offend those who feel differently about the food she is rejecting.

Q. *We have some good friends whom we often invite for dinner. Their teenager, time and again, does not eat the entrée but will eat an entire basket of rolls or the whole bowl of potatoes, leaving little or none for others. Her parents say nothing, but I get frantic seeing my balanced dinner being unbalanced by her eating habits. Do I have the right to say anything to her?*
A. Yes, although nothing you say will sound especially gracious. When you see that she is starting in on the roll basket, for example, ask that the rolls be passed to you. If she asks for them back, say, "Kate, these are all that are left and the people on this side of the table haven't had any yet." This is a form of public dressing-down and generally I don't approve of that, but if you are truly worried about your dinner being balanced for everyone, it is necessary to say

something. Better yet, if you indeed share dinner frequently and this has been her pattern, call her in a few minutes before everyone else and tell her that you know she really likes rolls, or potatoes, but that you have to be sure that there is enough for all the dinner guests. Try to provide a side dish that she does like, but teenagers should not be catered to by providing separate meals.

Q. I have a dear friend whose daughter interrupts us relentlessly when we are talking, whether it is at her house or mine. It is hardly worth trying to talk. Do I have the right to say something?

A. No, you do not. It is up to her mother to change this behavior. You do have the right to say, "Susan, I seem to be very distracted lately, but every time Amy interrupts us I forget my train of thought. Let's try to continue this conversation some other time." This, of course, will make Susan feel terrible, although if you make your comment gently she shouldn't also be angry. If she agrees with you and says she doesn't know what to do about it, you might suggest that she has to stop allowing her daughter to interrupt. The mother who invariably stops and says, "What is it, dear?" when her daughter interrupts is helping her to establish a habit that will do her a disservice all her life.

Q. How can I be sure that my children say "please" and "thank you" when they are visiting friends' houses?

A. The only way you can be really sure of this is if you yourself have made their use a habit and insisted that your children never forget to use them at home.

Beyond that, you, of course, remind them to "say thank you to Mrs. Adams when you leave," or "Remember to tell Mr. Geoffreys thank you for taking you to the game."

Q. *When we have family guests for dinner, is it all right to excuse the younger children from the table? My sister-in-law insists that they should remain with the adults, but their fidgeting and boredom is more distracting to me than excusing them.*
A. I believe that table manners should be the same for children as they are for adults, with one exception: Children should be permitted to be excused from the table, when very young, if the meal is an extended one. Expecting a young child to sit quietly through a protracted meal when his food is gone or when he is finished is an unreasonable demand on his patience and ability to sit still without wiggling, fiddling and noise-making to help pass the time. "May I please be excused?" should be asked of parents or of the hostess when dining with friends and relatives.

Q. *Do I have the right to ask a guest's children to be a little quieter if their mother doesn't seem to notice the noise they are making?*
A. You have the right if you have a reason for asking for quiet, such as thin walls in an apartment building so the neighbors are being disturbed, or a napping baby or your own inability to hear whatever conversation you are having in person or on the telephone, etc.

Q. When a child guest breaks one of my children's toys, should I ask his parents to replace it?
A. No, not if it was an accident. If he broke it willfully or purposefully, you have the right to tell his parents this and ask, under the circumstances, that they replace the toy. Tell them that you would not say a word if it had been an accident, but that since the child seemed to have no regard for your child's property, you feel it should be replaced. Be prepared for them to be angry, huffy and possibly distant in the future, however, since no one is pleased to hear his or her child accused of willful damage. They might even accuse you of being mistaken, but odds are they will replace the toy before they cross you off their social play date list!

Q. My daughter sometimes is invited by a friend and her family to go to the movies or out for ice cream or to an amusement park. I always give her money, but they invariably pay her way. How can I let them know that she has money and is prepared to pay her own way?
A. You can tell them that she has money for her admission or ice cream or ticket or whatever when they pick her up, and you can tell her to be sure to make the offer to pay for her costs. If they pay her way anyway, then be sure that she writes a thank-you note the next day. This is how she will learn to accept hospitality gracefully. You then should return the treat for your daughter's friend, by taking her to the movies or out for a treat some other time.

Q. *What things should I be teaching my children about behavior when we have guests, in addition to the boundaries they understand about interrupting, quiet and other usual expectations?*

A. Children should be taught to rise to meet an adult guest, to shake hands if the adult extends his or her hand and to maintain eye contact when speaking with someone. Children should not be seated again until the guest is seated, and should naturally give up a spot on the couch if there is nowhere else for the guest to sit. They should also be helped to understand the basics of conversation so that they do not, out of shyness, give monosyllabic answers when an adult is trying to engage them in conversation. They should also know how to excuse themselves from a conversation, a group or the dinner table, and learn that once excused, they are not to dally around the room but rather go to their own rooms or outside to play. Children should also learn to comfortably use an adult's title and name. It is far more polite to respond to a "How are you, Johnny?" with, "I'm well, thank you, Mrs. Patterson, how are you?" than "Fine, thanks," or worse yet, just "Fine."

Q. *My daughter will be turning three and has several new friends from nursery school. She would like a birthday party, with her friends in attendance, and has requested "party bags." What are party bags?*

A. In some communities, the birthday child gives her guests a small bag of gifts as a thank-you for attending her party. These gifts can be an assortment of candy, a jar of bubbles, a small toy that ties in with the theme of the party, stickers and other items beloved by children. This truly is a localized custom, so you might want to check with mothers of older children to see if this is a tradition in your area. If it is, the bags themselves can be purchased glossy gift bags or they can be brown paper lunch bags decorated by your daughter with stickers or crayon drawings. It is best to write each recipient's name on the bag so that there is no confusion, and to hand the bags to children as they leave the party rather than during the party when they tend to open them and lose some of the items within.

Q.When I am sleeping over at a friend's house and the whole family shares the bathroom, can I leave things like my toothbrush and toothpaste in the bathroom?
A. Wet things, like a washcloth, a just-used toothbrush and a bar of soap in a travel soap dish are best left neatly at the side of the sink. Other items, such as deodorant, your hairbrush and lotion or powder should be returned to your overnight bag so that they do not take up all the room on the sink top or counter.

Q. What should I do with something I can't chew when I am having dinner at a friend's house?
A. You should put your fork or spoon to your mouth, put your other hand over your mouth, and push the hard-to-chew piece onto the spoon. You then put it on the side of your plate. You should

never spit it into a napkin or directly onto your plate, nor remove it with your fingers.

Q. When I have friends over, I ask them if they would like something to drink. They always say, "I don't know," or "No, I guess not." I know they would really like something but don't know how to get them to say so. Is there a better way to ask?

A. It is much easier for someone to say yes when you give him or her a choice of selections rather than the choice of yes or no. Instead of saying, "Would you like something to drink?" say, "Would you like a cola, orange juice, or seltzer?" or whatever your choices are. You'll find that you'll get a much better positive response just by rephrasing your question.

Index

About the Author

Elizabeth L. Post, granddaughter-in-law of the legendary Emily Post, has earned the mantel of her predecessor as America's foremost authority on etiquette. Mrs. Post has revised the classic *Etiquette* five times since 1965. In addition she has written *Emily Post's Complete Book of Wedding Etiquette, Emily Post's Wedding Planner, Emily Post's Advice for Every Dining Occasion, Emily Post on Business Etiquette, Emily Post on Entertaining, Emily Post on Etiquette, Emily Post on Invitations, Emily Post on Second Weddings, Emily Post on Weddings, Please, Say Please, The Complete Book of Entertaining* with co-author Anthony Staffieri, and *Emily Post Talks with Teens about Manners and Etiquette* with co-author Joan M. Coles. Mrs. Post's advice on etiquette may also be found in the monthly column she writes for *Good Housekeeping* magazine, "Etiquette for Everyday."

Mrs. Post and her husband divide their time between homes in Florida and Vermont.